THE
𝕾iege 𝕺f 𝕵erusalem
BY TITUS.

Written by
THOMAS LEWIN, ESQ.
OF TRINITY COLLEGE, OXFORD, M.A., F.S.A.

1863.
Edited and Annotated, 2016, by Bradley S. Cobb

Cobb Publishing
www.TheCobbSix.com
2016

Please check out our website (TheCobbSix.com) for more books, and also the Jimmie Beller Memorial eLibrary for a growing collection of FREE eBooks (see more information on the back page of this book:
TheCobbSix.com/Jimmie-Beller-Memorial-eLibrary/

A Kindle edition of this book can be purchased inexpensively at Amazon.com

Printed in the United States of America.

ISBN-13: 978-1535444989
ISBN-10: 1535444983

Preface.

THE following Work originally consisted of three distinct Parts, all converging to the same point—the illustration of the topography of Jerusalem. However, the second and third parts were such that, even the author admitted, would not be interesting to most people. The second part was a journal of the author's trip to Jerusalem, describing the topography. The third part was a "General Sketch of the Topography," written prior to his visit to the Holy City.

To quote from the author's original preface:

"The idea of the First Part arose thus. It was felt that the 'General Sketch of Jerusalem' would, from its nature, yield but little entertainment; and it was feared that the journal would not prove much more attractive. If, therefore, the author wished to introduce his readers to a knowledge of the topography, it occurred to him that the best and only successful mode of doing so would be to interweave his subject with a narrative of sufficient interest to outweigh the dullness of the local details. The last days of Jerusalem, so graphically described by Josephus, appeared to possess the necessary requisites, and hence 'The Siege of Jerusalem by Titus.'

"If the author's prognostications be fulfilled, most of those who take up his volume will peruse the First Part; some will perseveringly find their way through the Second; and a few, imbued with antiquarian lore, or having made the holy places of Jerusalem their peculiar study, will struggle through the Third.

"The author, in these pages, has laid before the reader all the information which he has been able to collect from previous publications or personal observation; but it must be confessed that, after all, a great part of the topography of Jerusalem lies buried some five fathoms under the surface, and we must wait patiently until further discovery furnish materials for arriving at great precision."

Mr. Lewin acknowledged that most people wouldn't read his journal or his discussion of the topography of Jerusalem, and so we have decided not to waste space to republish what the original author was certain most of you wouldn't bother reading anyway.

However, the author has done us a great favor in giving us a condensed version of the Siege of Jerusalem (as described by Josephus), but with a particular emphasis on describing the topography, the locations where each of these events took place, and he also includes drawings of the layout of the city so we can better understand what took place, move by move, act by act in the tragedy that was orchestrated by God Himself to destroy the Jewish nation in AD 70.

Bradley S. Cobb
Editor, 2016.

Contents

THE SIEGE OF JERUSALEM BY TITUS.

Chapter 1.

When ye shall see Jerusalem compassed with armies, then know that the desolation thereof is nigh. Then let them which are in Judaea flee to the mountains; and let them which are in the midst of it depart out; and let not them that are in the countries enter thereinto. For these be the days of vengeance, that all things which are written may be fulfilled. . . . And there shall be signs in the sun, and in the moon, and in the stars; and upon the earth distress of nations, with perplexity; the sea and the waves roaring; men's hearts failing them for fear, and for looking after those things which are coming on the earth —Luke 21:20-22, 25-26.

In AD 70, and therefore thirty-seven years after the Crucifixion of our Lord, which was in AD 33, Titus, the son of Vespasian, and who had been left in command of the forces in Judaea on the elevation of his father to the Imperial purple, commenced his march against Jerusalem, the only city in which the rebellion, begun in AD 66, was still maintaining itself.

Titus at this time was in his twenty-ninth year. He did not exceed the ordinary height, but was well proportioned and strongly built. His countenance was lighted up with good-humor, and at the same time carried a dignified air that repelled intrusive familiarity. One of the most accomplished men of the age in literary and polite acquirements, he could speak and write well, improvise a *jeu d, 'esprit,* take down a speech in shorthand, and was so skillful in penmanship, that, as he said of himself, had he not been Emperor he might have made a first-rate Forger. He was not inferior in military prowess, for no one could draw the bow with such unerring aim, as on one occasion twelve of the enemy, transfixed by as many of his arrows, could testify. He was a good swordsman, as he had proved in many a hand to hand combat, and was particularly noted for dexterity in horsemanship. He had served as military tribune with credit under Vespasian in Britain, and had since commanded a brigade with equal or greater success in Judaea. If not entitled to rank with the great captains of antiquity, he was perfectly conversant with the art of war, and fully capable of conducting a campaign against a bold and resolute enemy. Titus, who was all amiability as Emperor, is said in these his earlier years to have leaned towards cruelty, and I fear that our narrative will furnish some substantial grounds for the accusation. As Emperor, also, he was a pattern of chastity, but in Judaea he became acquainted with the Cleopatra of the age, Berenice, the sister of Agrippa, King of Trachonitis, great-grandson of Herod, and they lived together until he ascended the throne of the Caesars, when deference to public opinion led to a separation, which is reported to have been a painful one on both sides. The rumor was rife that he had promised her marriage, but there was no tribunal which could award damages against a Caesar.

Of the forces at the disposition of Titus we can only form an approximate estimate, as Josephus has nowhere stated the exact amount. In the first place, he had four legions or regiments of the line, viz. the famous 10th, which had immortalized itself under the first Caesar in Gaul and Britain, now commanded by Larcius Lepidus; the 12th, which had somewhat tarnished its laurels by a precipitate flight from Jerusalem at the outbreak of the war in AD 66; the 5th, commanded by Sextus Cerealis; and the 15th, commanded by Titus Phrygius.[1] The strength of a legion was usually about 4,200, which would yield for the four legions 16,800. These were the regulars, but the Romans had also in their pay a large force of irregulars formed into cohorts. Under Vespasian there had been twenty-three cohorts, of which ten contained 1,000 each, and the other thirteen 600 each,[2] making together 17,800. It is impossible to say with any degree of certainty what proportion of these auxiliaries was present with Titus, as two Egyptian cohorts only, of 1,000 each,[3] are mentioned incidentally as commanded by Fronto Liturnius.[4] However, the siege of Jerusalem was the great event of the war, and the utmost resistance was to be expected, and I think we may assume (after allowing deductions for garrison duty in distant parts) that one half at least of the whole number, or 8,900, were

---

[1] Josephus, *Wars of the Jews,* 6.4.3; 5.1.6 (Note: each reference from this work of Josephus will simply be marked with the book, chapter, and paragraph number.)

[2] 3.4.2

[3] 3.4.2

[4] 6.4.3

assembled under the walls of Jerusalem.

Such was the amount of the regulars and irregulars of the Roman army proper; but besides these Titus had under his banners the contingents furnished by the various potentates of Syria, the feudatories of Rome, as by Agrippa, King of Trachonitis; Antiochus, King of Commagene; Sohemus, King of Emesa; and Malchus, King of Petra. In an earlier stage of the war, the first three had furnished each 2,000 foot, and the last 5,000 foot,[1] making together 11,000. At the present juncture the whole of these troops had probably been called upon to cooperate.

Hitherto we have spoken of the infantry, but Titus had also with him a considerable body of cavalry. Frequent mention is made of them in the course of the siege, and they were employed in repelling sallies, bringing assistance on sudden emergencies, scouring the country in search of supplies, and cutting off communication by the ordinary roads. Each legion had attached to it a squadron of 120 horse,[2] making together 480. Titus had also a body-guard of picked men to the number of 600.[3] Thirteen of the cohorts had been recently accompanied by squadrons of 120 each,[4] making together 1,500; and assuming, as in the case of the cohorts, that one half were present, we may reckon them at 750. Of the allies, it is mentioned in the course of the war that Agrippa, Antiochus, Sohemus, and Malchus had each furnished 1,000 horse,[5] making together 4,000; but as cavalry would not be so much in request as infantry at a siege, we shall allow only one half of these, or 2,000.

The sum total of the Roman army would therefore, upon a rough estimate, stand as follows:

Infantry	
Four legions of 4,200 each	16,800
Auxiliary cohorts in Roman pay	8,900
Contingents of the allies	11,000
Total	**36,700**

---

[1] 3.4.2; and see 2.18.9
[2] 3.6.2
[3] 5.2.1
[4] 3.4.2
[5] 3.4.2

Cavalry.	
Legionary squadrons	480
Body-guard	600
Squadrons of auxiliary cohorts	750
Squadrons furnished by allies	2,000
Total	**3,830**
Making a grand total of	**40,530**

These computations can scarcely be regarded as excessive. That the troops collected at Jerusalem amounted together to a very large force, may be inferred from the fact that they were able to erect a wall of circumvallation round the whole of Jerusalem, and five miles in length, in the course of three days. I am by no means sure that our estimate has not been considerably underrated, as we know that the Roman army in Judaea had not long before been computed by Josephus at about 60,000 men, besides camp followers.[1]

The King Agrippa, of whom we have spoken, was the Agrippa before whom and whose sister Bernice Paul pleaded with so much eloquence in the time of Festus, and who was *almost* persuaded to be a Christian. He had not the courage to forfeit his petty kingdom by refusing to serve against his country; but at the same time he was not so devoid of feeling but that his ignominious position at the side of Titus caused him some compunction. Not so, however, with the Jewish renegade Tiberius Alexander, the prefect of Egypt, who gloried in his shame. By renunciation of the faith of his fathers, and by abject flatteries and a plausible address mixed with considerable abilities, he had contrived to win favor at the court of Rome, and had risen to distinction. A bad man may be a good officer where interest does not conflict with duty, and in all the army there was no one on whom Titus had more reliance than on Tiberius Alexander. So much so that he was second in command under Titus, and no one contributed more to the downfall of Jerusalem than this artful and unprincipled timeserver.

There was in the Roman army at this time one descendant of

---

[1] 3.4.2

Abraham whose character has been the subject of warm discussion. By some he has been venerated as almost inspired, and by others he has been pronounced an accomplished rogue. By his own account he had taken a leading part in the rebellion, and commanded in Galilee; but the Roman power had been too much for him, and, after a gallant defense of Jotapata, he was made prisoner, but had recently been set free, and was now in attendance upon Titus as interpreter. We allude to Joseph, son of Matthias, commonly called Josephus, an eyewitness from first to last of the siege which we are about to describe, and who has furnished a graphic account of the horrible scenes of carnage and famine that ended only with the total destruction of the city. His pen may not have the Attic elegance of Thucydides, for he wrote in a foreign tongue, and he cannot lay claim to the character of an impartial historian, for Josephian hyperbole has become almost a proverb; but, allowing for exaggeration where the honor of his own countrymen or that of his imperial patrons is concerned, we may look upon his narrative as a tolerably faithful account of the actual occurrences. For the halo of light which the Wars and Antiquities have thrown upon the Christian religion we ought to be deeply grateful.

Had these works not come down to us, what a cloud of darkness would have hung over the birth and rise of Christianity!

Titus set forward on his march from Caesarea, the Roman capital of Palestine, about the beginning of April. He had then with him the 5th and 15th legions, and the auxiliary cohorts, and most of the allies. The 10th legion had been quartered during the winter at Jericho, in the plain of the Jordan, and the 5th at Emmaus, or Nicopolis, now Amwas, halfway between Jerusalem and Jaffa, and these two legions were to join him before Jerusalem on a day fixed. The order in which the army of Titus marched was this: first came the allies; then Titus and his body-guard; after him the cavalry; then the engines of war for the siege; the cohorts of auxiliaries; the legions or troops of the line, six abreast, with the eagle at the head; and lastly the baggage and the rear-guard.[1]

Titus directed his march through Samaria, and arrived about 10th April at Gophna, where he encamped. The next day he advanced to Gibeah of Saul, somewhat less than four miles from Je-

---

[1] 5.2.1

rusalem.[1] Gibeah of Saul was so named from its having been the birthplace and residence of the first King of Israel. It lay on the east side of the great north road, and was seated on a knoll or eminence, now covered with ruins, and called Tuleil el Ful.[2]

At Gibeah Titus halted his army, and, at the head of his body-guard of 600, set forward himself to reconnoitre. As he had no fear of encountering an enemy, he wore only his ordinary foraging cap, and was without any corselet. At the end of three miles he reached the crown of the hill called Scopus, or Belle-Vue, and here, all at once, Jerusalem and its environs lay unrolled, as on a map, before him. They were just one mile distant, but so clear and bright was the day that the doomed city seemed to lie at his feet, and to be already within his grasp. Jerusalem, as he gazed upon it, had a simplicity and compactness about it that indicated a city 'at unity with itself.' On the left or east it was bounded by the deep dark valley of Jehoshaphat, and therefore called Kedron, or the Gloomy; on the right or west and on the south it was girt in by the elbowing valley of Hinnom. On the north only was no ravine, for there, without the city, was a broad expanse, a *champ de Mars*, about half a mile square, encompassed on the north and east by the valley of Jehoshaphat, which here first runs from west to east, and then, turning southward, deepens as it descends towards the city. On the east side of Jerusalem, about half-way down, rose majestically to the skies, and glittered in the sun, the white terraces of the Temple, rising one above another, and crowned at the top with the Holy of Holies, the habitation of Jehovah. On the opposite or west side, about half-way down, frowned the formidable towers of the castle of David, the palace of Herod; and nearer to him, at the northwest corner of the city, was the Psephinus or Rubble Tower, the tallest and stateliest, though not the most finished, of all the bulwarks, the more conspicuous from its position on the highest and most commanding eminence. Titus dwelt upon the scene for a few minutes in silence, and perhaps cherished a hope, in the cause of humanity, that all this magnificence might become his without the destruction of the inhabitants; that he might take so goodly a hive without killing the bees: but the wrath of heaven was not to be thus appeased.

---

[1] 5.2.1
[2] Rob. i. 579

He now descended the hill of Scopus, and crossed the shallow valley of Jehoshaphat, running there from west and east, and ascended the open plateau at the north of the city. As he passed along the beaten road, he could not but admire the beautiful villas of the wealthy citizens that lined the sides, the orchards of olive, and gardens teeming with the fresh blossoms of spring. All was so calm and peaceful, that apparently he might continue his course up to the very Damascus Gate, flanked as it was by strong towers. Prudence, however, whispered that he was in presence of the enemy, and he turned off by a road to the right, which led in the direction of the Rubble Tower, at the north-west corner of the city. Titus and a few troopers had already left the main road, and the rest were following him, when suddenly a dark and dense column of men, at a rapid step, was seen pouring along the road, and before his guard could recover from their surprise, the thunderbolt was launched against them, and the body-guard was broken in two. Titus and his immediate comrades were intercepted in the by-lane, and the cavaliers that were still on the road, thinking that Titus was doing the same, wheeled about and fled. Titus was alive to the danger, and prepared for the worst. To ride across country to the camp was impossible, from the walls and gardens that like a network covered the whole space. To press on towards Psephinus might be to fall into a snare, and be carried he knew not whither. In a moment his mind was made up, and drawing his sword, and driving his spurs into his steed, he shouted to those about him, 'Comrades, follow me!' and dashed at once into the midst of the enemy. Javelins flew and swords gleamed. One trooper at his side rolled from his horse; another was dismounted and a prisoner; but Titus and the rest (thanks to the mettle of their horses and their trusty blades) forced their way unscathed through the throng, and rejoined the body-guard, now in dismay from discovering that Titus was not amongst them. The fact was, that the signal-men from the top of the Women's Towers, which flanked the Damascus Gate, had descried the approach of the little band in the distance, and a sally was ordered; and, from a bend in the road before the gates, the column had not been observed until it had pounced upon its prey.[1] This little incident gave Titus a wholesome taste of the desperate courage of the enemy, and served him as a

---

[1] V.2.2

lesson for all the remainder of the war. Had he been cut off on this, the threshold of the campaign, it is hard to say what might not have been the consequences. No one possessed the same authority as Titus over the legions, auxiliaries, and allies; and had jealousies and factions sprung up in the camp as in the city, Jerusalem might have escaped, as a bird from the snare of the fowler.

In the course of the night the 5th legion joined from Amwas, having made a long and fatiguing march by the route which falls into the great north road at Gibeah of Saul.

The next day Titus moved his army forward from Gibeah of Saul to Scopus or Belle-Vue, one mile from the northern wall of the city. The 12th and 15th legions were thrown forward and encamped together on the knoll half-way down Scopus; and the 5th legion, which had been marching the greater part of the previous night, were encamped three furlongs to the rear, that, in case of attack, the weary and worn regiment might not bear the brunt of the onset.[1]

Just as the troops were taking the measurements for their camp, the 10th legion also joined from Jericho, and was ordered to camp on Mount Olivet, to the east of the city, and at the distance of three quarters of a mile from it.[2]

———

Before proceeding further, we must glance at the state of matters *within* the walls of Jerusalem. The city at this time was in the hands of three despots, who, while they were all hostile to the Romans, were all waging an internecine feud with each other.

First and foremost stood Simon Bar-Gioras, a native of Gerasa.[3] Josephus has portrayed him as a bloodthirsty tyrant; but the brush of Josephus could blacken at one end while it could varnish at the other, and Simon had at least some redeeming qualities: a man to be feared rather than loved, and yet capable of warm affections; and woe to him who offered any affront to the wife of his bosom, who partook his counsels and shared his dangers. He could shed blood, even that of his dearest friends, but it was only when stern necessity required it at his hands: of powerful frame, and inured to arms, he had won the confidence, if not the affections, of the soldiery, and in

---

[1] 5.2.3
[2] 5.2.3
[3] 4.9.3

the hour of danger every eye was turned towards Simon. He aspired to dominion, not by chicanery, which he scorned, but by the strength of his arm and the good blade that it wielded. He would have trampled on the liberties of his country, but he bore the hatred of Hannibal to the Romans, who oppressed it. Had he been the sole master of Jerusalem, he might have checkmated the ponderous assault of Titus, but the city was enveloped in the poisoned tunic of faction, and at last committed suicide by lifting its own hand against itself.

Simon was absolute master of the High Town or Upper Market, the ancient Jebus; the south-west hill surrounded by the valley of Hinnom on the west and south, and by the Tyropaeon valley on the north and east, and enclosed by the first or earliest wall. He also held the whole of the third wall, that of Agrippa; which, commencing from Hippicus, the tower at the north-west corner of the High Town, ran northward to Psephinus or the Rubble Tower, and then deflected eastward to the valley of Jehoshaphat, and then turned southward to the Temple Platform. This gave him the command of Cenopolis or the New Town, both the Upper on the western and the Lower on the eastern hill. But within the third wall and at some distance from it was the second wall, which beginning from the Gate Gennath in the north wall of the High Town, bent round to the north-east corner of the Temple Platform; and the quarter enclosed within this wall, the inner Low Town or inner Acra, was divided between Simon and John of Gischala. Simon also occupied the greater part of the wall which commencing from the south-east corner of the High Town ran along the steep of Ophel, overlooking the valley of Jehoshaphat, to the south wall of the Temple Platform; and by this means he was dominant over the inferior part of the Outer Low Town, or Outer Acra on Ophel, and in particular had in his power the fountain of Siloam at the southern foot of Ophel, a prize of high importance to a city seated on the plateau of a thirsty mountain.

Simon was at the head of 10,000 native Jews and 5,000 Idumeans, all well-equipped from the arms which had been stored up by Herod, or had been wrested from the 12th legion of the Romans at the outbreak of the war. His headquarters were in the Palace of Herod, now the castle of David, at the north-west corner of the High Town; and he resided in the main tower of the citadel called

Phasaelus, from the summit of which he commanded a view, not only of the city, but of all the adjacent country.[1]

———

The next in importance to Simon was John of Gischala, one of those rank weeds that are occasionally brought to the surface from the lowest depths of humanity by the storms of civil strife: a man intent upon his own selfish ends, and striving to gain them by flatteries and deceit; ever ready to shed the blood of those who stood in his way; ambitious of leadership, but still more eager in the pursuit of pelf.[2] A bandit in his earlier days, he had learned to endure hardship and even to look death in the face without flinching. Less stalwart than Simon, he had greater activity, and had a ready supply of artifices that made him a match for any opponent. John, by these arts, had constituted himself the head of the extreme faction called the Zealots, and was now master of the Temple Platform, the middle Low Town, or middle Acra, and some parts of the city immediately adjacent, both on Ophel to the south and in the inner Low Town on the west. No less than 6,000 men drew the sword at his bidding. His orders had been formerly issued from the Palace of Grapte, in the outer Low Town on Ophel,[3] but he had since been driven from it into the Temple Platform. Open and deadly war had been long waged between him and Simon, and the intermediate parts of the city that lay as neutral ground upon the confines of their respective territories had, from their repeated sallies and raids upon each other, become a smoking ruin and a desolation. The stores of provisions which had been carefully collected for years against the siege, were ruthlessly burnt amid these reprisals; and Josephus hesitates not to say that the capture of the city was brought about at last, not by the force of arms but by the dreadful famine caused by this insane destruction of the sinews of war.

———

The hydra of faction had yet a third head, Eleazar, son of Si-

---

[1] Phasaelus still remains, and I have looked from it on the same hills that Simon did; but alas! the splendours of the city have sunk into the earth and lie entombed many fathoms below Jerusalem that is.

[2] Dishonestly-gained wealth.

[3] 4.9.11

mon,[1] a man of sacerdotal lineage, but without any of the principles or feelings which should have animated one so well descended. Goaded by ambition, he had taken from the first a leading part in the rebellion, and had led the Zealots: outwitted by John, he had seen that artful plotter exalted over his head, and regarded as the leader of the Zealots themselves; and stung by envy, and disgusted with John's duplicity, he had formed a cabal, and collecting about himself 2,000 attached followers had seized on the Inner Temple. John tried in vain to bring back the schismatic by fair words, and then commenced open war, but with no better success. The Inner Temple was a quadrangular terrace that rose out of the middle of the Outer Temple, the court of the Gentiles. It was ascended by flights of steps, and was surrounded besides by a high wall with a cloister or colonnade, from the roof of which the soldiery had free play. Thus the inferiority of Eleazar in numbers was compensated by the superiority of his position. Incessant conflicts had been waged, and at the arrival of Titus were still going on between John and Eleazar, and the altar above and the court of the Gentiles below had been defiled by the blood of human victims. Despairing of taking the Inner Temple by assault, John had sacrilegiously availed himself of the timber collected for the repairs of the Temple, and begun to build towers which would reach to the summit of the Inner Temple wall; but at this juncture the Roman legions appeared on Scopus and disconcerted all his schemes.

As for the people, the quiet dwellers in Jerusalem, they adhered to no party, and were the prey of all — sheep that were first shorn, and then brought to the knife. Their houses were forcibly entered; their goods plundered; tortured to confess treasures which they did not possess, and put to death or spared just as the wind blew. The multitude said to have perished by these atrocities, and from the famine which soon followed, is too vast to be credited.

Besides the ordinary population of Jerusalem, there was at this time a countless throng of pilgrims waiting for the Passover. This was to take place on the 13th of April, but it was the custom of the Jews to arrive a week before to make preparation. Josephus would have us believe that 2,500,000,[2] or even occasionally 3,000,000,[1]

---

[1] 5.1.2
[2] 6.9.3

were congregated at the capital during the great festivals; but, allowing a large margin for exaggeration, and remembering that in disturbed times the attendance would be comparatively small, we may still suppose that the population at this season would be double of its usual amount. The floors of the houses within the walls were crowded, and without in the valleys and on the sides of the hills the ground was dotted with tents, while numbers of the poorer sort slept in the open air under their gaberdines or blankets.

The festivals were the fairs of the nation—the great gatherings for the transaction of business and the interchange of good offices. But now one universal gloom overspread the whole community. Hitherto, from intestine troubles, the Romans had neglected Jerusalem, but all men felt that the day of reckoning was at hand. In this state of suspense and excitement every little incident out of the ordinary course had its significance and increased their fears. A strange light at three o'clock in the morning had shone about the altar and temple, and this had been interpreted as a warning of conflagration. At another time, at midnight, the Corinthian or Beautiful Gate of the Temple, which had been closed at sunset by the united strength of twenty men, had opened of its own accord, as if to let in the enemy. Voices had been heard from the Holy of Holies saying, 'Let us depart hence.' War chariots and armies in battle array had been observed in the clouds.[2] And for the last year there had been hanging, and still hung, in the skies over Jerusalem, a comet which assumed the appearance of a flaming sword. Even so far back as before the outbreak of the rebellion, a poor half-crazed person — Jesus, the son of Ananus — had perambulated the city, uttering one incessant and doleful cry, 'A voice from the east, a voice from the west, a voice from the four winds of heaven, a voice against Jerusalem and the Sanctuary, a voice against bridegrooms and brides, a voice against all the people.' This had continued until it was deemed a nuisance, and he was taken before the magistrates and scourged, but still the same wail was heard from morning to night in the streets. He was then carried before the Procurator, and

---

[1] 2.14.3

[2] In certain states of the air, objects upon the earth are reflected on the sky; and on this occasion the Jews may have seen the Roman forces advancing upon Jerusalem reflected in the clouds.

his flesh almost tom from his body by the lash, but he only ex-claimed at each stroke, 'Woe, woe to Jerusalem!' Discharged by the Procurator as a maniac, he then again went about the city as before, with the wonted lament, 'Woe, woe to Jerusalem!' He noticed no one, and spoke to no one. He had no curses for those that beat him, and no blessings for those that fed him. Instead of passing for a person without his wits, he was now thought to be the mouthpiece of the Deity, and the populace, wherever he appeared, was filled with terror.[1]

Men's minds were in this morbid frame when the panic cry arose that the Roman eagles were on Scopus. Then was the striking of tents, and the rush of fugitives seeking for safety in flight; groups of men, women, and children were seen hurrying here and there, and stumbling against each other. The wiser and more long-sighted turned their backs on the city, and left it to its fate; in particular, it is said that the Christian Jews, warned by the prophetic words of their divine master, 'fled to the mountains' (for the ordinary passes were guarded), and retired to Pella. But the great mass of the people precipitated themselves within the walls, and were thus caught in a snare from which they afterwards attempted in vain to extricate themselves.

Now that the enemy was at the gate, it was time to think of de-fense, and the three chiefs, Simon, John, and Eleazar, met in con-clave, or at least communicated with each other through envoys, and exchanged pledges that until the common enemy were disposed of all intestine feuds should be sunk in oblivion; in other words, that while each maintained his position, he should lend a hand to repel the common foe.

No sooner had the compact been made than it was called into action. We left the Roman Legions busily occupied in pitching their camps, the 5th, 12th, and 15th Legions on Scopus, and the 10th on Olivet. Why this one legion should have been thus separated from the rest it is difficult to divine; perhaps for the convenience of the commissariat, or perhaps for keeping a more watchful eye upon the proceedings in the city, as the combined view from Scopus on one

---

[1] Bell. vi. 5, 3. He continued this unceasing wail until, in the course of the siege, he was heard to say, 'Woe, woe, also, to myself!' when he was struck down by a shot from one of the enemy's engines.

side, and from Olivet on the other, completely overlooked Jerusalem in all its length and breadth.

The sight, however, of one legion posted by itself, and employed upon entrenchments, invited an attack, and a sally was resolved upon. A watchman was posted on the eastern wall to signal by the waving of a mantle when to charge and when to retire, and, this matter arranged, the troops of John and Eleazar sallied out of the Golden Gate in the middle of the Temple Platform, and the troops of Simon out of St. Stephen's Gate, the only portal on the east side of the new city, and contiguous on the north to the Temple Platform. The united forces rushed down the valley to the Kedron, and rapidly ascended the opposite hill, and before the 10th Legion could form in rank, the Jews were upon them. A fierce conflict ensued, but eventually the legionaries were forced out of their half-formed entrenchments, and retreated over the hill. Immediate intelligence had been carried to Titus, and he at once started off with a chosen body to the relief of the 10th Legion, and arrived just in time to save it from destruction. The Jews were driven down the hill, but on re-crossing the Kedron the vantage ground was again on their side, and they re-formed and presented a bold front. Neither party chose to renew the combat, and Titus, after waiting some time, ordered the 10th Legion to re-ascend the hill and proceed with the encampment. No sooner had they commenced their retrograde march than the watchman on the walls, taking it for a flight, waved violently his mantle—the signal for a charge— when the Jews dashed forward with such fury that they broke the Roman line and drove them up the hill in confusion. Titus implored and threatened, and even drew his sword upon the fugitives, in the vain attempt to check the panic, but all in vain. Meanwhile the 10th Legion, on their way upwards, had heard the shouts, and, seeing the disorder, faced about, and charging downhill, restored the fight. The Jews resisted manfully, but the acclivity was steep, and they were hurled into the ravine, and sought safety within the walls of the city.[1]

The treaty of amity between the three despots now recoiled upon the head of one of the parties to it. The morning of 13th April dawned, and at noon the sacrifices for the Passover were to be killed. Eleazar was in possession of the Inner Temple and the altar,

---

[1] 5.2.4

and the worshippers who had come to Jerusalem applied for admission, and Eleazar, who was himself of the tribe of Levi, acceded to the request. But the insidious John of Gischala, who had solemnly sworn to drop all hostilities within the walls during the siege, regarded the oath as a convenient instrument of fraud, and seeing Eleazar lulled into security, determined on a step for the advancement of his own interests. He selected certain of his followers whose features were not familiar to Eleazar, and attired them in the garb of pilgrims, but at the same time armed them with swords and daggers, hidden under their gabardines. The unsuspecting Eleazar allowed them to pass with the rest, and no sooner were they in the Inner Temple than they made an onset with their weapons, and opened the gates to their comrades. An indiscriminate slaughter of Eleazar's partisans, and even of the innocent worshippers, followed. The end however was attained, for John, by this perjury and treachery, under the cloak of religion, regained possession of the Inner Temple, and the faction of Eleazar ceased. Simon and John remained alone upon the stage to fight, first with the Romans, and then, if they survived, with each other. It is singular that the life of Eleazar himself was spared. There must have been strong motives for lenity, or John could not have refrained from the gratification of spilling his blood. Perhaps John could not dispense with the services of Eleazar's surviving partisans, and these could only be purchased at the price of their leader's safety.[1]

The only assailable parts of the city were the northern and so much of the western wall as extended from the Jaffa Gate to Psephinus or the Rubble Tower, at the north-west corner. On all the other sides were the tremendous precipices of the valleys—viz., the valley of Hinnom on the west and south, and the valley of Jehoshaphat on the east. The weak line from the Jaffa Gate to the Rubble Tower, and thence eastward to the valley of Jehoshaphat, was protected by the wall begun by Agrippa ten years after the Crucifixion, and completed by the Jews in a hasty manner after the outbreak of the war in AD 66. This wall, now commonly called the Third Wall, was anciently known as the Great Wall, from its superior breadth and the dimensions of the towers. Had Agrippa perfected the wall as he commenced it, the city would have been impregnable, but the

---

[1] 5.3.1

jealousy of the Roman Emperor Claudius interdicted the work.

Titus was satisfied, from the vigorous sallies already made by the Jews, that he had no child's play before him, but must make his approaches against the city upon the most approved plan. As the assault, therefore, must be either against the north wall, or that portion of the west wall which lay between the Jaffa Gate and the Rubble Tower, he thought it indispensable for his safety, in the first place, to clear the ground opposite these parts, so as to afford a ready transit for his troops from one quarter to another. Posting, therefore, select bands to counteract any sortie[1] from the gates, he employed the rest of his army in levelling the suburbs. Houses were thrown down, walls demolished, fruit-trees and shrubs felled and removed, projecting rocks cut away, and hollows filled up.

Such a work of devastation, the conversion of ornamental scenery into a desolate battle-field, strongly stirred the passions of the besieged. How could they look upon such havoc? Why did not the people rise *en masse* against the despots that oppressed them, and open the gates to the Romans, who at least could not exercise greater barbarity than was inflicted by their present masters?

It seemed at one time as if some such *emeute*[2] within the city had broken out, for as the troops of Titus were clearing the ground on the north, the walls were seen lined with citizens who extended their arms to the Romans, and sued for peace, and implored them to take possession of the city. The war-party apparently had been overpowered, for at the same time a crowd was ejected from the Damascus Gate, and were in a state of the wildest despair, sometimes advancing to the Romans, and then, as if afraid of their sworn enemies, retreating again toward the city, but saluted on their approach with a shower of missiles from the walls. Titus had suspicions of an ambush, and commanded the soldiers to stand fast, but the battalion that was nearest the gate was under an irresistible impulse, and rushed up to the open portal to take possession, when the people, who had pretended to be outcasts, suddenly drew their concealed swords and attacked the Romans in the rear, while others sallying from the gate assailed them in front, and at the same time javelins, arrows, and stones were poured upon them from the two flanking

---

[1] an attack made by a small military force.
[2] an act of starting.

towers of the gate, called the Women's Towers. The Romans, from very shame, fought with desperation, but numbers were slain, and the rest were chased all the way along the north road as far as the tombs of Helen, now the tombs of the kings; and the Jews on their return brandished their shields, and danced and skipped and made grimaces in mockery of the Romans for the way in which they had been befooled. Josephus tells us that the tombs of Helen were three furlongs from the wall,[1] but according to recent admeasurement the interval is just four furlongs, or half a mile, and it seems, therefore, to have been lucky that the Jews were not intercepted in their retreat; but probably there was no other battalion under arms nearer than at the Jaffa Gate, and the mass of the army were engaged with the pickaxe and shovel. We need not suppose, however, that the Jews pursued the enemy all the way to the tombs of Helen, but only that the Romans did not stop their precipitate flight until they had reached that monument.[2]

The Roman army was occupied upon the clearance of the ground for four days,[3] and on the completion of the work Titus took measures for moving his camp nearer to the city. About two furlongs to the north of the Rubble Tower was the highest point of the plateau to the north, and here the 12th and 15th Legions, under Titus, formed their united camp. At the Jaffa Gate, the valley of Jehoshaphat coming up from the south turned in a north-west direction, and at the head of it was the Serpent or Dragon Pool, now the Mamilla, and a little to the east of the pool, where still is a cemetery, was the tomb of Herod Agrippa, the father of Agrippa who was now with the Roman army. A little to the south, and opposite the Jaffa Gate, and at the distance from it of two furlongs, was a knoll, and here the 5th Legion, under Sextus Cerealis, formed their encampment.[4]

When the ditches and walls of the two camps had been completed, the next step was to transport thither the engines of war and baggage; and from the excessive precautions taken by Titus, it is plain that he entertained a very wholesome respect for his resolute

---

[1] Josephus, *Antiquities of the Jews*, 20.4.3
[2] *Wars of the Jews,* 5.3.3
[3] 5.3.5
[4] 5.3.5

adversary. A cordon was drawn round the north and west sides of the city, consisting of men under arms stationed no less than seven deep. In front were the legionaries three deep, then a rank of archers, and behind them the cavalry also ranged three deep. The Jews could not venture a sally against such a living wall, and the engines and baggage were safely conveyed along the rear from Scopus to the two newly-constructed camps. The 10th Legion was not moved, but retained its position on Mount Olivet.

Now that the legions were located in permanent quarters, Titus had to consider where he should deliver the assault. He therefore mounted his charger, and, attended by a guard, and also by Nicanor and Josephus, who were well acquainted with the city and its inhabitants, rode round the wall. In the course of the reconnaissance, Titus, out of compassion, turned to Nicanor and said, 'Go near and offer them terms.' Nicanor and Josephus, with a flag of truce, approached the wall, when an arrow flew and struck Nicanor on the left shoulder. A spirit like this left no alternative but to prosecute the siege.

The result of the survey was this. The High Town, or south-western quarter of the city, could not be taken and held without possession of the Palace of Herod, now the Castle of David, the fortress at the northwest corner of the High Town; and the Low Town, or Acra, could not be taken and held without possession of the Temple Platform, the fortress of the Low Town; but the Palace of Herod was impregnable from without, by reason of the deep valley of Hinnom on the west, and the Temple Platform was impregnable from without, by reason of the still deeper valley of Jehoshaphat on the east. But if Titus could only take the outer or third wall, which ran from the Jaffa Gate northward, and so round to the Temple Platform, he would then be able to approach the Palace of Herod from the north, and the Temple Platform also from the north.[1] The third wall and the second wall may be regarded as two concentric segments of circles, resting on the Palace of Herod on the west, and on the Temple Platform on the east. The diagram will show the different localities, with their relative positions.

---

[1] 5.6.2

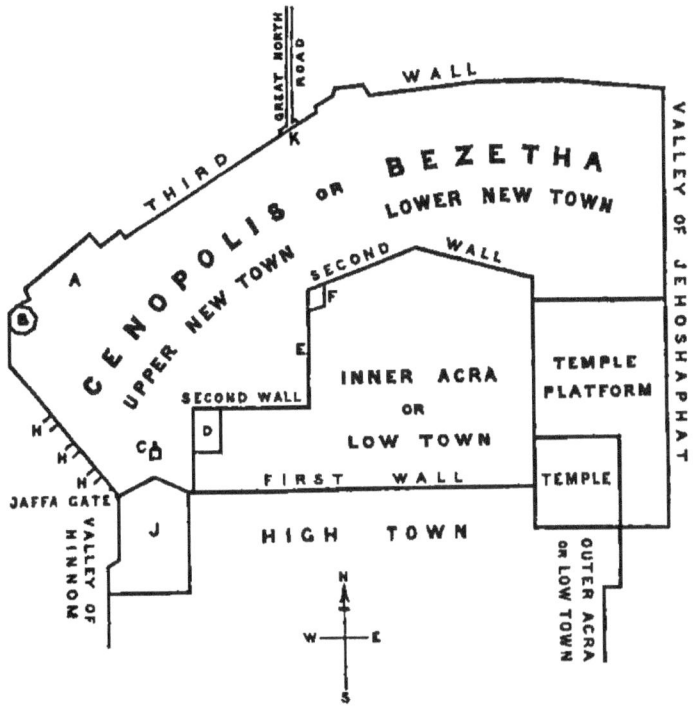

A. The camp of the Assyrians.
B. The tower Psephinus.
C. The monument of the High Priest John.
D. The Pool of Hezekiah.

E. The present Bazaars.
F. The middle tower of the second wall.
H. H. H. The three mounds erected against the outer or third wall.

Having decided on attempting, in the first instance the capture of the outer or third wall, as preliminary to the assault on the two fortresses, the Palace of Herod of the High Town, and the Temple Platform of the Low Town, Titus had now to choose between the northern side of the third wall and that part of the western side which lay between the Jaffa Gate, and Psephinus or the Rubble Tower at the north-west corner. In former ages the assaults of the enemy had invariably been directed against the north, and on this side therefore the fortifications were strongest. Not only was the wall exceedingly massive, but at the foot of it was a deep and wide fosse,[1] where the wall itself did not stand upon a rock of inaccessible height. On the west the wall was not of equal proportions, nor was the fosse so deep or broad, and the reason perhaps was that the valley of Je-

---

[1] A wide trench, usually filled with water, like a moat. It was used for defense.

hoshaphat might be thought to offer some protection. However, the valley coming up from the south turns off at the Jaffa Gate in a north-west direction, and leaves a triangular level space between the valley and the western wall (the Jaffa Gate forming the apex), and this intermediate area was of sufficient width for the operations of a besieging army. The valley itself, also, was so shallow here as to offer no impediment to the transit of troops. Titus therefore determined on making the assault on the western side of the city, over against the monument of John the high priest, which stood just within the third wall, a little to the west of the Pool of Hezekiah, then called the Almond Pool.[1]

The wall was too high for an escalade,[2] and was therefore to be breached. The artillery for this purpose was the battering-ram, an immense mast with an iron headpiece in the form of a ram's head, whence its name, and slung by ropes or chains from upright timbers uniting at a point over the engine. It was then projected with all the force that could be given to it by a gang of soldiers against the wall, and such was the shock that no masonry could long withstand its repeated blows. But before the ram could be brought into play it was necessary to fill up the fosse, and as the upper part of the wall was the weakest, it was usual to mount the ram upon a bank or platform, so as to strike the wall at some height from the ground. The construction of the bank, and the playing of the ram was a work of great difficulty and danger, for, of course, those who manned the walls were all the time pouring down volleys of javelins, arrows, and stones. Those who wrought at the bank or the ram were therefore to be put under cover, and for this purpose hurdles, armed with wet skins as a prevention against fire, were stretched overhead. But again, unless the wall were cleared of those who manned it, sandbags would be let down to break the stroke of the ram, or a fragment of rock would be sent down big enough to break off the ram's head. To counteract these obstructions a wooden tower was commonly employed by the besiegers. It was of considerable height, say 75 feet,[3] and of corresponding breadth. It was constructed at a distance from the wall, or at least out of reach of shot, and was then pushed

---

[1] 5.6.2
[2] An attack using ladders to scale a wall.
[3] 5.7.1

upon wheels up or along the bank until it neared the wall. As the enemy would send against it arrows and javelins carrying combustible materials for setting it on fire, the sides, except that at the rear, which could not be reached by the enemy, were protected by iron plates. The tower consisted of several tiers or stories, well supplied with scorpions,[1] catapults, and ballists, which poured showers of missiles through the open windows, or apertures, against the enemy on the wall.

On 22nd April, Titus began the work by distributing his army into three divisions, and ordering each to erect a bank, mount a ram, and construct a tower.[2] A vast quantity of timber was required, not only for the battering-rams and towers, but also for the banks, which were composed in great measure of woodwork. Every tree, therefore, in the neighborhood of Jerusalem was now felled;[3] and Josephus breathes a sigh as he relates how the environs of Jerusalem, which before resembled a paradise, were thus utterly denuded and became a desolation.[4]

> Now while with toil unwearied rose the mound,
> The sounding axe invades the groves around;
> Light earth and shrubs the middle banks supplied,
> But firmer beams must fortify the side;
> Lest when the towers advance their ponderous height,
> The mouldering mass should yield beneath their weight.
> Rowe's Pharsalia.

As the three banks proceeded, those who wrought at them were not only protected by hurdles overhead, but on each side were stationed javelin-men and archers, in front of whom were arranged scorpions, catapults, and ballists. Some of the ballists were of extraordinary power, for those of the 10th Legion could throw a stone of 1 cwt. the distance of two furlongs,[5] and Josephus mentions that at Jotapata a stone from one of the ballists carried off a man's head

---

[1] a 'scorpion' is a precursor to the modern crossbow, and was considered a sniper's weapon.

[2] 5.6.2; 5.7.1

[3] 5.6.2

[4] 6.1.1

[5] 5.6.3

and projected it three furlongs.[1]

The soldiers of Simon, meanwhile, on the wall were not idle. They possessed a few engines of war, partly taken from the stores of the Romans in Antonia at the outbreak of the rebellion, and partly captured from the 12th Legion when chased from Jerusalem to Bethhoron, but the Jews had no experience in the use or management of the engines, and they were of little use; but the archers and slingers were numerous and skilful, and gave great annoyance to the besiegers.

The way in which the Jews defended themselves from the Roman ballists is singular. A watchman with a quick eye could see the white stone as it flew in the air, and immediately cried out 'The chiel's coming,' when the group separated and threw themselves on the ground. The Romans soon discovered this maneuver, and painted the stone black, when, being lost to the sight, it did much more execution.[2]

The banks were now approaching the wall, and the workmen, who did not dare show themselves beyond the covering hurdles, threw out a plumbline, and measured the distance, and found that the rams could reach the bulwark.[3] Upon this, the battering-rams were advanced, and slung upon the three banks, and were then driven with tremendous force and with the noise of thunder against the wall. The whole city was scared at the reverberation of the echoes from the three batteries, and ran about wild with terror. Even Simon and John were brought to their senses for the moment, and combined their troops against the common enemy. Flaming brands were thrown in showers from the walls upon the besiegers below, while others made sallies, and attempted to fire or break in pieces the covering hurdles. But wherever the Romans were hotly pressed, Titus hurried up with cavalry and archers, and drove the Jews back. At the end of the first day's assault, the only injury done to the wall was, that a corner of one of the towers had been broken off by the ram of the 15th Legion.[4]

On the west side of the Palace of Herod, the citadel at the

---

[1] 3.7.23
[2] 5.6.3
[3] 5.6.4
[4] 5.6.4

north-west corner of the High Tower, was a secret postern,[1] which had not been observed by the Romans. Simon, whose head-quarters were in Phasaelus, the principal tower in the citadel, could, from the summit of it, watch every movement of the enemy, and seizing a favorable moment, when they were off their guard, he poured out his troops through the secret gate, and so took the legions by surprise that they gave way, and the Jews followed furiously in the direction of the works, in the hope of firing them. An obstacle often arises when least expected, and just as the Jews had reached the goal, the Alexandrian auxiliaries made a stand. They were not comparable, in general opinion, to the legions; but on this occasion the courage of the legions seemed to have migrated into the swarthy troops of the Nile. This saved the works, for while the conflict was raging, Titus, who was ever on the alert against accidents, galloped up with his chosen cavalry, and drove the Jews back into the city. The historian adds that Titus, on this occasion, slew no less than twelve men with his own hand! if so, he displayed rather the valour of the common soldier than the caution of the commander; but if Josephus really believed this, we can only say *Credat Judaeus.*[2] One of the gallant Jews was taken prisoner, and Titus, most cruelly and meanly, caused him to be crucified under the walls, that his agonies on the cross might break the courage of his comrades.[3]

Hitherto the wooden towers built by the Romans had not been brought to bear, but they were now completed, and were moved forward upon the banks; but the first result was somewhat inauspicious. At midnight a tremendous crash was heard,—the alarm was sounded, and the whole army was in a panic, the men running here and there, and challenging each other in the dark for the watchword. Titus started from his couch, and was soon on the spot. The towers, from their great height and size, were of enormous weight, and the earth, or wood-work, of one of the banks, had sunk or given way, and the tower, with all its armament of engines, had fallen to the ground.[4]

---

[1] A small rear entrance or gate at the back of a castle.

[2] A Latin phrase, whose meaning, paraphrased, is "Tell some other Jew, I don't believe it."

[3] 5.6.4-5

[4] 5.7.1

No sooner were the two remaining towers brought against the wall, than the Jews were fairly overmatched. It was the triumph of engineering skill over sheer courage. The portholes and embrasures of the towers sent out such a volley of arrows, javelins, and stones, that no one could stand upon the wall and live. The battering-rams had now full play, and their force quite amazed the Jews, who had never before witnessed the effects of military engines of the highest class. One ram, in particular, excited their admiration, and was nicknamed by themselves Nicon, or Conqueror; and it was Nicon at last that brought down the wall against which it butted. A breach being effected, the forlorn hope dashed in, and the Jews fled in terror behind the second wall.[1] It must be confessed that at this, the last pinch, the Jews did not display their wonted energy. At Jotopata, for instance, when the Romans stormed, the Jews poured boiling oil over the advancing enemy, which, searching the body through the crevices of their armour, made them writhe with agony. And again, when the Romans laid down the scaling planks for the soldiers to cross, the Jews had dashed down a flood of melted grease, so that the combatants lost their footing, and rolled about in all directions. But *now* the besieged fled at once behind the next wall, and Josephus attributes this want of spirit partly to the incessant fatigues which they had already undergone; partly to the vacillation arising from the divided counsels of the factions; but more particularly to a persuasion on the part of Simon's partisans, that the third wall was of the less consequence, as two walls would still be interposed between them and the enemy—that is, the High Tower was protected by its own wall, the first, and beyond that, by the second wall, except at Herod's Palace where the fortifications were deemed impregnable.[2] No doubt the design of Titus had been, after capturing the third wall, to assault the Palace of Herod at once between the third and second walls; but the Jews believed, and they were right, that the strong towers, Hippicus, Phasaelus, and Mariamne, which crowned the northern brow of the cliff on which the palace stood, would bid defiance to any force that Titus could bring against them.

The fall of the outer or third wall was on 7 Artemisius, or 6th

---

[1] 5.7.2
[2] 5.7.2

May, the 15th day from the actual commencement of the works, and about a month from Titus' first arrival.[1] Thus ended the first act of this bloody tragedy.

---

[1] 5.7.2

Chapter 2.

'After threescore and two weeks shall Messiah be cut off, but not for himself: and the people of the prince that shall come shall destroy the city and the sanctuary; and the end thereof shall be with a flood, and unto the end of the war desolations are determined'—Daniel 9:26.

THE quarter of which Titus thus became master was, in the Jews' language, Bezetha; or in Greek, Cenopolis; and in plain English, the New Town. The shape of it (see illustration, prior chapter) may be compared to a triumphal arch resting on two bases, viz., at the west on the Palace of Herod, and at the east on the Temple Platform. The second wall, which formed the concavity of the arch, commenced on the west, from the eastern end of the Palace of Herod, or rather from the Gate Gennath near it, in the northern wall of the High Town, and swept round in an irregular curvilinear form to the western end of the Temple Platform. Cenopolis was intersected by the Asmonean valley, which descended southwards from the Damascus Gate, and thus divided it into Upper Cenopolis on the west, and Lower Cenopolis on the east. This new suburb had first spread itself on the eastern hill by the population gradually extending itself to the north of the Temple. The western hill was never much inhabited, and the reason seems to have been that in that part there was a cemetery, and the Jews had a religious horror of a graveyard. The tomb of John the High Priest, near the Pool of Hezekiah, was a leading feature in the localities of the city throughout the siege; and a little to the north of it was the tomb of our Lord, now the Holy Sepulchre, and in the same vicinity are still to be seen two other tombs, hewn in the rock in the old Jewish fashion. The thinness of the population was the cause, according to Josephus, why this quarter had not been comprised within the city when the second wall was built.[1] Agrippa, ten years after the Crucifixion, had attempted to encompass it by the third wall; but an interdict from Rome put a stop to the work, and Cenopolis was not

---

[1] 5.6.2

brought within the city until the completion of the third wall by the Jews, at the outbreak of the insurrection in AD 66. In the Upper Cenopolis on the western hill was the area, called the Camp of the Assyrians, so named from its having been the site of the Assyrian encampment in the time of Sennacherib. The spot was at the north-west corner of Cenopolis, the highest ground.

Titus, that he might be nearer the scene of conflict, now moved his own camp from the plateau at the north of the city to the camp of the Assyrians, between the third and second walls. The 10th Legion still remained on Mount Olivet, and the 5th on the knoll opposite the Jaffa Gate; and as the new camp within the city was small,[1] we may infer that part only of the 12th and 15th Legions were brought thither from their united camp on the north. Titus, however, had with him a strong force, and one which is described as reaching all the way from the camp of the Assyrians on the west, to the valley of Jehoshaphat on the east. The reason of this extended front, no doubt, was that they might be retired to such a distance as to be inaccessible to the shot from the second wall.

Titus had supposed that when once master of the outer or third wall, he could at once, without taking the second wall, operate against the Palace of Herod on the west, and the Temple Platform, guarded by Fort Antonia, on the east; and he now proceeded to carry this plan into execution. The details are not given, but it is evident that the Romans won no laurels, or we should have heard more about it. The soldiers of Simon manned the north wall of the High Town between the second and third walls—that is, from the tomb of the High Priest John, at the junction of the second wall with the wall of the High Town, as far as to the Watergate in the Tower of Hippicus, at the north-west corner of the High Town; and John, on the east, manned the north wall of the Temple Platform. The soldiers of Simon were devoted to him, and now that his stronghold, the Palace of Herod, was attacked, they fought with the utmost fury. The contest before and upon the walls raged from day to day, and even at night both sides slept under arms. John, on the other side, was

---

[1] This appears from the circumstance that the tribunal of Titus, when he distributed the rewards, was erected, not in the camp within the city, which would not contain the members, but in the camp on the plateau on the north of the city.— 7.1.2.

equally resolute in the defense of his fastness, the Temple Platform; and Titus was forced at last to confess that the two citadels were impregnable, unless he could first master the second wall, and so make his approaches upon more favorable ground.[1]

It was therefore resolved, as the next step, to storm the second wall. The quarter enclosed by it was the Inner Low Town, or Inner Acra, and it somewhat resembled in its configuration a quadrant; the second wall, from the Palace of Herod on the west, to the Temple Platform on the east, forming the arc; while the two sides were the north wall of the High Tower on the south, and the western wall of the Temple Platform on the east (see earlier illustration). This part of Jerusalem was in strange contrast to the New Town enclosed by the third wall, for while large tracts of the New Town were scarcely inhabited, and only sprinkled with houses few and far between, the Inner Lower Town was perhaps the most populous of the whole city. It was not honored by the presence of the aristocracy, for all the palaces were either in the High Town, or else in the Outer Low Town, on Ophel below the Temple. In the High Town were the Palace of Herod on the west, the Palace of Agrippa on the east, and the Palace of the High Priest on the south; and on Ophel were the Palaces of the royal family of Adiabene, the Palace of Queen Helena in the middle, and the Palace of Grapte to the north, and the Palace of Monobazus on the south. In the Inner Low Town, enclosed by the second wall, on the contrary, were located the artisans and merchants and shopkeepers. The streets and lanes were narrow and crooked, and were a perfect labyrinth. The ground itself was uneven, as the Asmonean valley ran down it from north-west to south-east; and the ascent from the valley was pretty steep, both on the eastern and western sides. The habitations were lofty, but mean as compared with those in the High Town or Outer Low Town. In short, the Inner Low Town was the heart of the city, the most thickly peopled, and bore all the marks of an overloaded quarter straitlaced for room, and unable to expand itself beyond the confining walk.

The point selected for the assault was the middle Tower of the north wall, where were the wool-mart and clothes'-mart and the braziers' shops,[2] and where to this day are the bazaars. The batter-

---

[1] 5.7.3
[2] 5.8.1

ing-ram was soon brought into play, and a strong body of archers cleared the battlements for those that manned them. The second wall was not so strong as the outer or third wall, which had been already taken, and the ram soon caused the Tower to totter. The officer in command there under Simon was one Castor, and when the fall was evidently approaching, all, with the exception of Castor and ten others, abandoned the fortress. The scene that follows reads more like a puppet-show than a page in history.

The Tower was of the ordinary character, having a vault or guardroom below, and a breastwork above with battlements. Castor and his men lay crouched behind the breastwork until the Tower began to tremble, when Castor stood up and threw out his arms towards Titus in earnest supplication, and offering to surrender unconditionally. The heart of Titus was touched with compassion, and he promised to spare Castor his life. At the same time the other ten rose up, and were seen engaged in a deadly feud, five of them crying out for pardon, and the other five shouting no surrender, and assaulting the five dastards. Their heads only were visible to the Romans above the breastwork, but swords gleamed in the air, and every now and then was the ring of a weapon upon the breastplate, and a man dropped. All this was a make-believe. They only dashed the hilts of their swords against their own corselets, and then pretended to fall dead. Castor meanwhile sent a message to Simon not to hurry himself, for he could make fools of the Romans for some time longer. At this point, an arrow flew from a Roman bow, and struck Castor by the side of the nose. He coolly drew out the shaft, and held it up in silent reproach to Titus, who sternly rebuked the archer, and bade Josephus go up to the wall and grant their lives. Josephus, who knew his countrymen better, excused himself; but Castor was at this time calling lustily for someone to come up and catch the bag of gold which he had brought with him. Aeneas, a deserter, ran to the foot of the Tower when Castor threw down, not the bag of gold, but a fragment of rock, which missed Aeneas himself, but nearly killed the person standing next him. Titus now saw through the cheat, and ordered the battering-ram to be applied without mercy. Just before the Tower fell, Castor set fire to it, and escaped with his comrades through the vault, and made the Romans believe that they were miracles of patriotism, choosing to perish in the flames rather than surrender to the enemy.[1]

The breach was effected on 11th May, and the Romans immediately took possession of the second wall. As the Inner Low Town was of no great extent, Titus entered by the breach with his body-guard only, and about 1,000 legionaries. The inhabitants of this quarter being exclusively the common people, who would gladly have freed themselves from the yoke of the tyrants and have surrendered to the Romans, Titus gave orders that none should be slain who did not carry arms, and that the houses should not be destroyed. He even went so far as to promise a restoration of their property to all peaceful citizens. This conduct, the result of compassion or policy, was interpreted by the tyrants as a sign of weakness, and the soldiers of Simon, threatening death to any that uttered the word surrender, made a desperate onset, meeting the Romans face to face in the streets, and throwing missiles upon them from the housetops, and, from an intimate knowledge of the byways and alleys, falling upon the flanks of the enemy where least expected. At the same time, also, a sally was made out of the High Town by the nearest gate; and the Romans on the second wall, finding their enemies on both sides of them, escaped from the wall and fled to their camp. Meanwhile the Jews pressed the Romans very hard within the city. Titus, never anticipating such an attack, had incautiously omitted to widen the breach, and the consequence was that the Romans were pent up in narrow lanes, and were unable to extricate themselves through the opening by which they had entered. In this strait they fought with desperation, and eventually Titus, bringing up a body of skillful archers, and posting them in commanding positions, the Jews were checked, and the Romans were enabled to retire through the breach. Thus the Jews, having lost the second wall, again recovered it; and were so elated by this temporary triumph that they imagined themselves already victors, and asked each other whether the enemy would dare to renew the attempt. For three entire days did Simon and his followers hold the second wall, and hedge round the breach with a living rampart of bodies; and the force of the whole Roman army could not dislodge them. On the fourth day, however, the 14th May, the strength of the Jews was exhausted, and inch by inch they were forced into the

---

[1] 5.7.4

High Town, and Titus now became finally and absolutely master of the second wall and the quarter enclosed by it, the Inner Low Town.[1] So ended the second act of this bloody drama.

---

[1] 5.8.1-2

Chapter 3

*'There shall be famines, and pestilences, and earthquakes,' and,
'Then shall be great tribulation, such as was not since the beginning
of the world to this time, no, nor ever shall be.'—Matt 24:7, 21.*

TITUS had unfortunately omitted, on the capture of the second wall, to widen the breach, and he had suffered a severe disaster in consequence; but now that he had again retrieved his loss, he took care to prevent a recurrence of it, by throwing down the whole of the northern limb of the second wall. The western limb, or at least the southern part of it, which joined on to the first wall of the High Town, he left standing, as it would facilitate his operations in assaulting the High Town.[1]

The troops had suffered much from the street-fighting of the last four days, and Titus now gave them a little rest. The periodical time for paying the army had arrived, and Titus took the opportunity of making the ceremony an imposing pageant. This he calculated would have a beneficial effect, by encouraging his own army from the consciousness of its strength, and by intimidating and disheartening the enemy, if it did not at once lead to a surrender. Both infantry and cavalry were ordered to clean and burnish their arms, and then, fully equipped and in full uniform, to present themselves for the receipt of their pay. The tribunal was erected on the north of the city, and the various bodies marched past in succession. First came the Legions, with their plumed helmets and metal breastplates, carrying a spear in the right hand and a buckler in the left, with a long sword girt on the left side and a dagger on the right. Then came the auxiliary Cohorts, some with the Roman armament, others with long bows and quiver of arrows, and others with their slings and pouches of leaden bullets. Last, but not the least notable, advanced the cavalry, every one lance in hand, and leading his horse gaily caparisoned. Such was the immense force collected, that for four consecutive days the living tide flowed past. So gorgeous a spectacle could not fail to attract the admiration, if not to work upon the

---

[1] 5.8.2

fears of the besieged; and Fort Antonia, and the northern side of the Temple, and the north wall of Sion, and, indeed, all the roofs of the houses, were thronged with spectators, looking with beating hearts and bated breath at the multitudes banded together for their de-struction. At the same time, so calmly and orderly was the display conducted, that a stranger, looking down from Mount Olivet, might have imagined the pageant a scenic representation, and that the few feet of wall between the two hosts was the conventional barrier that divided the assembled masses of the citizens from the performers on the grand stage of the plateau on the north.[1]

The imposing ceremony came to an end, but failed to produce the desired effect. There was no sign of submission; and Titus had again to let slip the dogs of war. The Inner Low Town enclosed by the second wall, of which he was now master, constituted only about a third part of the Low Town, otherwise called Acra. The main part of it, and that which commanded the two wings, was the Temple Platform, or Middle Acra. Without the possession of this, the Inner Low Town on the west could not be held in safety; and if the Temple Platform were captured, the Outer Low Town to the south was no longer defensible. The Temple Platform, however, was a citadel of extraordinary strength. About 1,500 feet long from north to south, and 900 feet wide from east to west, it was surrounded on all sides by a high and broad wall, and not only so, but on it stood the famous fortress Antonia, upon which Herod had lavished enormous sums to make it impregnable. The Temple itself, also, which rose below Antonia in successive terraces one above the other, was in itself a little citadel not easy to be taken. The area of the Temple Platform was thus distributed: at the south-west corner, and occupying a square of 600 feet, was the Temple itself, encircled by cloisters; from the northern cloister ran out two colonnades, about 400 feet apart, which connected the Temple with Antonia on the north. Still more to the north, and above Antonia, and at the north-west corner of the platform, had originally stood the Macedonian Acra or Castle, which had given its name not only to the Temple Platform, but to the whole of the Low Town, including the two wings, the Inner Low Town to the west, and the Outer Low Town to the south. The Acra, however, had been razed by the Asmoneans, and the site of it was

---

[1] 5.9.1

now a castle-yard attached to Antonia, with a tower at the north-west corner, still called the Acra, after the name of the celebrated Macedonian fortress, but incapable of defense towards the south against an enemy in possession of Antonia.

Neither the Temple nor Antonia reached all across the platform to the east; but the open space between them and the eastern wall is referred to by Josephus as the *so-called* Cedron ravine, a phrase to distinguish it from the valley of Jehoshaphat, which he calls simply the Cedron. On the outside of the platform on the western side were two pools, one commencing from the northwest corner of the Temple, and running along the foot of the wall for a space of 84 feet. This still remains, and is called the Mekhimeh Pool, and is now, and perhaps always was, arched over, and therefore more properly a great cistern than a pool. More to the north of this, and a little to the west of the wall of Antonia, was another large pool, which is still traceable, called the Struthion or Soapwort Pool, a name given to it from the extensive lavatories about it, and which are still carried on in the immediate neighborhood.

Titus, on capturing the third wall, had obtained access to the north of the Temple Platform, which was not covered by the second wall, and he had attempted, as we have seen, without mastering the second wall, to carry the Temple Platform by assault from the north; but the bulwarks there had defied him, and he had desisted in despair. Now that he held the second wall and the Inner Low Town, he prepared to assail the western wall of the Temple Platform from the west side, where the wall, as looking toward the city and protected by it, had not been constructed with the same massiveness.

Titus distributed his army into two divisions, and ordered one of them, consisting of the 5th and 12th Legions,[1] to throw up two banks against Antonia, one of them about the middle of the Struthion or Soapwort Pool, and the other at the distance from the first of 30 feet.

---

[1] 5.11.4

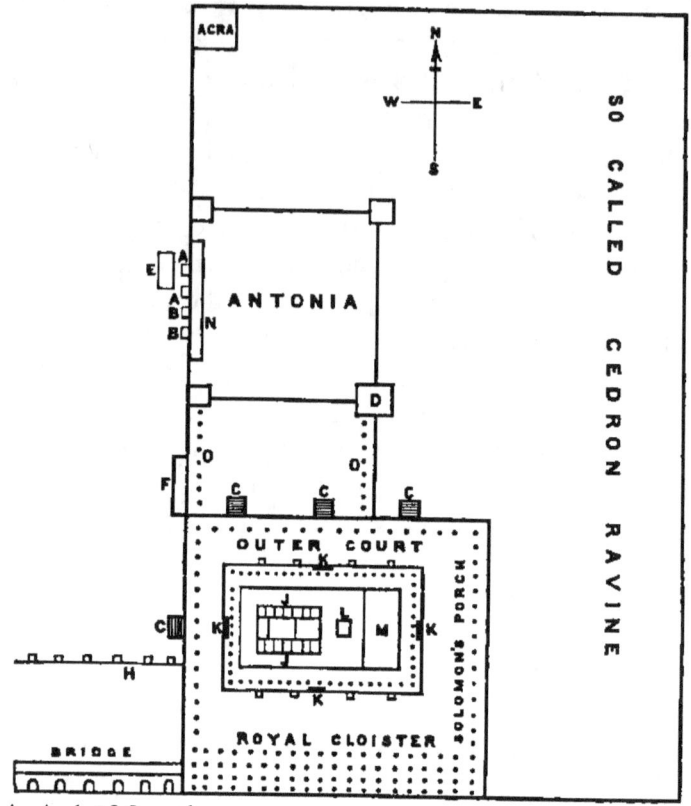

A. A. 1st Mounds.
B. B. 2nd Mounds.
C. C. C. C. 3rd Mounds.
D. Main Tower of Antonia, now site of the Mosque of Omar.
E. Struthion Pool.
F. Mekhimeh Pool.
H. Junction of the First Wall,
J. J. Inner Court.
K. K.K.K. Alcoves.
L. Altar.
M. Court of Women.
N. 2nd Temporary Wall.
O.O. Connecting Cloisters.

To keep the Jews in check, by dividing their attention, Titus ordered the other division of his army, the 10th and 15th Legions, to proceed against the High Town. The main citadel—the Palace of Herod—was defended on the north by the three towers of Hippicus,

Phasaelus, and Mariamne; and as Titus, when master of the third or outer wall, could approach these on the north in the space between the third wall and the second wall (see Illustration 1), he had attempted, on the capture of the third wall, to carry the citadel by assault before taking the second wall, but he had been completely foiled by the amazing strength of the fortifications. He had since mastered the second wall, and being now more sanguine of success, he employed the 10th and 15th Legions in throwing up two banks against Herod's Palace. The second wall, which had been purposely left standing in this part, lay between the Almond Pool (now the Pool of Hezekiah) on the east and the tomb or monument of John the High Priest on the west. The 10th Legion was commanded to throw up a bank at the Almond Pool, and the 15th Legion at the High Priest's monument.[1] The engines of war disposed upon the second wall would thus be a protection to the works on either side.

The banks against Antonia, and also those against the High Town, proceeded but slowly, for by this time the Jews had learnt the art of constructing engines, and, what was more important, the art of using them. They had now three hundred scorpions for throwing arrows, and forty ballists for casting stones;[2] and the effective way in which they worked them so galled the Romans, that only Roman endurance would have persevered.

As much time would be consumed before the works could be completed, Titus during the interval made another essay to induce the besieged, whose resources were daily dwindling, to surrender without further contest. The negotiator selected was the historian Josephus, who had sense enough to see the hopelessness of the Jewish cause, and eloquence and address enough to plead with his countrymen in the most acceptable form. He was also personally interested in bringing about the immediate cession of the city, for on taking command in Galilee at the outbreak of the war, he had been obliged to leave his family as hostages in Jerusalem; and his father, mother, and wife and children were all now in the hands of the despots.[3] Josephus proceeded on his arduous mission, and posting himself so as to be out of reach of shot, but within hearing, repre-

---

[1] 5.11.4
[2] 5.9.2
[3] 5.9.4; 5.13.3

sented the impolicy, and even the impiety, of continuing a struggle that could only lead to the destruction of the city and Temple. By some he was merely derided; but others vented the most dreadful execrations against him, and some even assailed him with missiles.[1] The populace would willingly, from the miseries they were suffering, have opened the gates; but Simon and John, who were in possession of the walls, were inexorable, and the unarmed multitude were a helpless flock of sheep environed by a pack of ravenous wolves.

Jealously as the people were watched, many who had no domestic ties to keep them in the city contrived to evade the sentinels and desert to the Romans. Before starting upon the venture they would sell their little all for a gold coin, which they swallowed, that on being stripped by the Romans it might not be discovered. The greater part of those who thus came over were allowed to go free; and happy the lot of such as could turn their backs on the Holy City.[2]

The horrors that now began to be enacted are truly appalling. Was anyone thought to have treasure? The mere suspicion cost him either his life or his livelihood: for he was forthwith brought to a mock trial and suborned witnesses charged him with treason, viz., an intention of deserting to the enemy; and condemnation to death, or at least the confiscation of goods, immediately followed.[3]

But scenes of this kind were only the commencement of iniquity. When provisions ceased to be sold in the market, the armed brigands went about the city, breaking into private houses and carrying off all that could be found. If the inhabitants were emaciated, they were allowed to starve; but if in good case they were put to the most excruciating tortures, to make them discover their secret stores.[4]

Persons that had only themselves to care for sold their goods for a handful of wheat or barley, and then retired into some remote corner to swallow it. Such as attempted to make it into bread were driven by the cravings of hunger to eat it half-baked.[5]

---

[1] 5.9.4
[2] 5.10.1
[3] 5.10.2
[4] 5.10.3
[5] 5.10.2

Families reduced to extremities barricaded their doors, and sat down to their last meal; and often as they were thus engaged armed ruffians would burst open the bars and locks, and rush in for the plunder, when a death- struggle followed. Old men were dragged by the beard, and women by the hair; and children, instinctively clutching a morsel of food, were ruthlessly dashed against the stones.[1]

The poor, of course, suffered most; and where nothing remained to sustain life, the father (as his wife and children were pledges for his return) was allowed to pass the gates at night to gather a few herbs from the suburbs, but on his return the heartless guard of the gates robbed him of all he had collected, and sent him home empty to perish with his family.[2]

The number that straggled from the walls at night— some, the brigands with arms in quest of plunder, and others, the citizens in search of sustenance—must have been prodigious, if we can credit the statement that five hundred in a night were made prisoners by the Romans.[3] And how were these poor wretches treated by Titus, 'the pet and darling of the human race?' They were scourged and tortured, and then crucified before the walls—nay, mockery was added to their sufferings, for the Romans amused themselves by inventing novelties in the art of cruelty. Some were crucified erect, some head downwards, others sideways, and others in any posture that relieved for the moment the ordinary monotony.[4]

The object of all this inhumanity was to intimidate those who remained, and force them into surrender. But Simon and John gave out that the crucified were not the prisoners of war, but the deserters; and for a time this ruse had the effect of preventing attempts to escape; but Titus upon this amputated the hands of the prisoners, that they might be unserviceable for war, and then sent them thus mutilated into the city to inform their countrymen of the fact.[5]

All was to no purpose, for Simon and John still resolutely maintained their position; and the desperate bands that fought under

---

[1] 5.10.3
[2] 5.10.3
[3] 5.11.1
[4] 5.11.1
[5] 5.11.2

their banners still remained faithful—to Simon through fear, and to John through the hopes inspired by his artifices.

About this time arrived in the camp Antiochus Epiphanes, son of the King of Commagene. He brought with him his guards, the finest of all the Commagene regiments, and called 'The Macedonians,' from their being armed after the fashion of Alexander's famous father. They were picked men, and in the prime of life, and full of courage. Young Antiochus himself had never experienced misfortune, and thought the world must bend before him, and was loud in his surprise that the siege should have lasted so long, as it was now about six weeks since the commencement. Titus calmly replied that there was a clear stage and no favor, and that Antiochus was at full liberty to try his luck. Antiochus upon this carried his Macedonians to the assault; but alas! they little knew the determined and now skillful enemy with whom they had to deal. They advanced with a bold front and rushed up to the wall, but, little used to actual warfare, and unprepared for so vigorous a resistance, they were hurled back in confusion, and throughout the siege we hear no more of the Macedonians.[1]

The banks against the Temple Platform had been commenced on 11th May, and at the end of seventeen days, i.e. on 28th May,[2] they were brought to completion. The engines of war, the scorpions, catapults, and ballists were now advanced to the front, and the rams, slung under the iron-sheathed hurdles, began to play upon the wall. At this moment a low rumbling sound was heard from below, and then, with a mighty crash, the mounds, as if by magic, sunk into the earth.

A cloud of dust arose, and was followed by a sulphurous smoke, as from the bottomless pit, and then flames bursting up, enveloped engines and men in one vast canopy of fire, and the banks were swallowed up and the engines of war consumed. John, in despair of checking the progress of the works by open force, had driven mines under the wall of the Temple Platform into the heart of the banks; and, supporting the earth as he proceeded with wooden props, had excavated the substratum, and filled the cavities with pitch and bitumen and combustible matter; and just as the battering-rams

---

[1] 5.11.3
[2] 5.11.4

commenced their work, John gave the order to fire the mines, when the banks of the Romans, which had cost them so many weeks' labor, were at once and for ever annihilated.[1]

Titus looked for better success with the two other banks against the High Tower; and after two days brought up the battering-rams, under the protection of the iron-sheathed hurdles, flanked by the engines of war. Simon had not the fertile invention of John; but he had more true courage, and a more devoted soldiery. Of all the valiant men that fought under him, none were of a fiercer spirit than Tephthaeus and Megassarus. These two, with a band of followers of the same mettle, made a sally from the gates of the High Tower with burning brands, and, amid a storm of missiles from the engines, rushed to the banks, scaled the sides, and before the Romans could stop their headlong course, set fire to the protecting hurdles. The enemy ran up to save at least the battering-rams, and struggled hard to rescue them from the flames, but the desperate assailants would not let go their prey, and, regardless of themselves, held the rams in the flames until the work of destruction was complete. Animated by this success, and increasing in numbers, the soldiers of Simon drove the Romans before them, and pursued them to their very camp. Here, however, they met with a check. It was part of the Roman discipline to post a cohort by way of guard in front of the camp, and not a man of them might move a step in retreat, or he was doomed to certain death. This advanced guard now stood firm, and formed a barrier against the surging tide, and at the same time the troops within the lines mounted the engines of war upon the walls, and plied the Jews with missiles. Titus, at the moment of the sally, had been occupied at Antonia reconnoitering the ground for the erection of fresh works in that quarter, but the shouts of the combatants were heard, and at the head of his chosen troops he hurried to the scene of conflict, wheeled round his force, and took the enemy in flank, and, other troops also hastening up to his assistance, he at length forced the Jews back, and drove them with considerable loss into the city. The great object, however, had been accomplished, for the engines and rams, and all the wooden framework of the banks, had been consigned to the flames.[2]

---

[1] 5.11.4
[2] 5.11.5

These successive disasters, first before Antonia and then before the High Tower, were a heavy blow and great discouragement to the Romans, and Titus called a council of war to deliberate upon future measures. The boldest were of opinion that the whole army should advance simultaneously against the walls, that the attention of the enemy might be distracted, and a breach effected somewhere. Others, more cautious, advised that, notwithstanding the present failures, the surest way was to proceed with banks and the battering-ram as before. Others argued that the assault should be turned into a siege; that famine must sooner or later bring about a surrender, and that to offer battle to desperate men, who, if left alone, could not hold out much longer, was a foolish and useless expenditure of human life.[1]

Titus listened with composure to these opposite counsels, and then struck out an independent course of his own, which eventually entailed upon the besieged the most fatal results. His proposal was to surround the whole city by a wall of circumvallation, so that all communication with the country might be effectually cut off, and all supplies from it intercepted.

This plan was adopted, and forthwith the whole army was divided into separate bodies, and the work distributed amongst them. The wall began from the camp of the Assyrians, in the Upper Cenopolis, where Titus had pitched his tent, and was carried eastward to the Lower Cenopolis, on the eastern hill, and then across the Cedron or Valley of Jehoshaphat, and ascended a little way up the Mount of Olives. It then turned southward, and continued along the slope of the mount to the Peristereon or Columbarium, the sepulchral caverns at the village of Siloam, and thence, still southward, to the foot of the Mount of Offence, where it crossed the valley near Enrogel or the Well of Job, and ascended the hill of Evil Counsel, and passed westward by the tomb of Annas the High Priest and Pompey's camp, and then turned northward along the west side of the Valley of Hinnom to the hamlet of 'Terebinths,' and on the east side of the Dragon or Serpent Pool (now Birket Mamilla), bent round the tomb of Herod eastward, and so reached the camp of the Assyrians, whence it had commenced.[2]

---

[1] 5.12.1
[2] 5.12.2

The whole length of the wall was forty stades, or five miles, and on the outside were constructed thirteen forts, the united circumference of which was ten stades;[1] and yet, such was the zeal and rivalry of the different sections of the army, that the whole work was completed in the space of three days. The Jews, indeed, offered no interruption, for their numbers were so diminished that they could no longer take the field. They could make a sudden sally from the gates against the works nigh at hand, but the wall of circumvallation had been withdrawn to a respectful distance, and had the Jews left the cover of the walls to assault it, their retreat would infallibly have been cut off by overwhelming numbers, and not a man probably would have returned to tell the tale.

As the circumvallation had been originated by Titus, he was anxious to secure its success; and on its completion sentinels paced all night between the towers to prevent a surprise; and during the first watch, from 6 to 9 P.M., Titus himself made the circuit to see that all were doing their duty. The second watch, from 9 P.M. to midnight, was committed to the renegade Tiberius Alexander, the second in command; and the two other watches were entrusted to the commanders of the legions.[2]

Now that the city was hedged in by this impassable barrier, and the scanty supplies which had before been furtively obtained after dark from the environs, were intercepted, the spectral form of famine began to rear itself in the city in its most hideous aspect. Women and children, at the last gasp, lay upon the roofs of houses; old men were found dead in the streets; and youths haunted the market-place with glazed eyes, and bodies distended from inanition; others crawled to their own graves, and lay themselves down, waiting for the hand of death. The stench from the carcasses became insupportable, and it was ordered that they should be carried out of the gate, and thrown into the valley of Hinnom, which now justified its name of Gehenna, a hell upon earth. Here, rotting and putrifying, lay heaps upon heaps of dead bodies, one vast mass of corruption,

---

[1] As the wall was apparently in the line of the third or outer wall of the city on the north, and ran along the farther sides of the valleys of Jehoshaphat and Hinnom, and yet was only forty stades long, how could the city, which lay within the valleys, have been so much as thirty-three stades in circumference?

[2] 5.12.2

running with ichor, and poisoning the surrounding air.[1] As Titus looked upon this dreadful sight, he held up his hands to heaven, and protested that not to his charge were these horrors to be laid.[2]

Simon and John, though death stared them in the face, relented not. Though the struggle was apparently hopeless, they would not allow the word 'Surrender' to be mentioned. Simon had been originally introduced into the city by Matthias, and was therefore beholden to him for his present elevation; but when Matthias and his four sons were found to have opened a communication with the Romans, he and three of his sons (for the fourth escaped) were seized, and at once executed. The father implored, as a favor, that he might be slain the first, but even this was denied him, and his three sons were butchered before his face, and then he, too, was decapitated.[3]

Among the officers of Simon was one Jude, who had the command of a tower in the north wall of the High Tower, and not far from the keep of Phasaelus, in which Simon had his headquarters. Jude, seeing the desperate state of the city, concerted with ten of his comrades, upon whom he could rely for secrecy, to open the gates to the Romans, and so save the remnant of Jerusalem. The next morning Jude, on different pretexts, sent away all his men who were not accomplices, and then shouted to the Romans to hasten up, and take possession of the wall. The Romans had so often been deluded, that they suspected a trick, and it was only after a long pause that Titus was convinced of the sincerity of the invitation, and ordered up a troop to the tower. This delay was the ruin of the plot. Simon, who was near at hand, got wind of what was passing, rushed with his guard to the spot, seized Jude and his fellow-patriots, executed them in the sight of the Romans, and flung their mangled bodies over the rampart. Savage and even brutal as was Simon, and insidious and crafty as was John, one can scarcely withhold the meed of admiration at the desperate obstinacy with which they thus fought the Romans inch by inch. The wonder is, how they could still maintain their authority, and instil the same indomitable spirit into the mass of their followers; but it must be remembered that, of the distress

---

[1] 5.12.3
[2] 5.12.4
[3] 5.13.1

and famine which we have described, the principal victims were the people. The armed soldiery had hitherto staved off the evil by breaking open the houses, and plundering the wretched inhabitants of all that could support life. As for John, he had sacrilegiously seized on the stores of the Temple, and distributed among his followers the large supplies of wine and oil devoted to the sacred services. But provisions were at length exhausted, and the partisans of the two tyrants were now beginning to sink themselves under the pangs of hunger.

Notwithstanding the jealousy with which the gates were watched, and the horrid tortures inflicted on the discovery of any leaning toward the Romans, desertions increased from day to day. Some, under pretense of making a sally, issued from the gates, brandishing their arms, and raising the shout of battle, and then went over to the enemy. Others, at the risk of their necks, dropped from the walls. Escape but too often ended in death; for in their famished state, they seized on the proffered food with avidity, and so over-loaded their stomachs as to burst asunder. But the great majority fell victims to the avarice of the soldiery. In Jerusalem money was plentiful, but there was nothing to purchase. The deserters were accustomed, before starting, to swallow their gold to avoid being plundered, and when the Romans discovered this, they ripped open the fugitives in cold blood, to extract the treasure concealed in the intestines. In one single night no less than 2,000 persons are said to have been thus slaughtered.[1] The Syrians and Arabians were the principal offenders; but even the Legionaries participated, and Titus could not prevent it. The evil, however, partly cured itself; for when it became known that the deserters were inhumanly murdered, those who remained preferred famine in the city to butchery without.[2]

Titus had now so cooped up the enemy that he had only to rest on his arms, and surrender or desolation must soon follow. He deemed it, however, beneath the dignity of the Roman name to wait ingloriously for the work of time, and being at the head of so numerous an army, he thought himself called upon to make another attempt at storming the enfeebled city. He had before directed his efforts simultaneously against both the High Town and the Temple

---

[1] 5.13.4
[2] 5.13.5

Platform; but the banks against both had been destroyed. He now contracted the area of his operations, and concentrated his whole force against the Temple Platform. Four new mounds, of extraordinary size, and all against the western wall of Antonia, were ordered to be erected. The great difficulty was the want of materials, for the trees in the suburbs had been consumed for the previous works, and the Romans were obliged to fetch their timber from a distance of eleven miles and upwards.[1]

John saw the banks gradually rising against Antonia, and yet, from the power and constant play of the Roman engines of war, he could not prevent their progress. He had before succeeded in undermining the *two* mounds; but, with diminished numbers, he could not grapple with the *four*. He looked forward, therefore, to the day when the wall would be battered down, and, to provide against such a catastrophe, he exerted himself to raise a counter-wall behind the first, so that the Romans, when they had breached the first, would be met by a second.

The mounds had been commenced on 7th June, and were now drawing towards their completion, when John determined upon a sally. This was an enterprise of great danger and difficulty, for the Romans, from their repeated losses, had become over-cautious, and the banks were protected by powerful war engines, and a heavy mass of troops were kept continually under arms, ready at a moment's warning to meet an assault. The Jews issued from the gate, but whether it was that they were badly officered, or that famine had broken their spirits, they did not from the first present that solid and compact appearance that augured success. On the contrary, they were seen swerving from side to side, and falling into detached parties; and while some went boldly on, others hesitated. Every step increased the confusion, from the showers of missiles that darkened the air from the scorpions, catapults and ballists that hedged in the works. The column became more and more unsteady, and at last, without having even reached the banks, they turned about and fled tumultuously back into the Temple Platform.[2]

The battering-rams were now planted upon the banks, and began to butt against the wall, but the spirit of the Jews upon the ramparts,

---

[1] 6.1.1
[2] 6.1.3

made amends for their pusillanimity in the field, for they poured down such a volley of stones and other missiles, that the battering-rams were prevented from taking much effect.

Seeing what little progress was made, the Romans had recourse to what they called the testudo or tortoise, that is, they advanced against the wall with their shields over their heads, the rear rank kneeling so as to form a slanting roof, and then the foremost rank plied the crowbar to wrench out the stones. They succeeded in dislodging four, but still the wall defied their efforts, and stood firm. Darkness overtook the combatants, and the Romans retired, with broken spirits at the result of the day's labor.[1]

The night brought them a piece of good luck, which amply compensated for the failure of the day; silence reigned in the camp and in the Temple Platform, when the wall, which had been undermined by John, and since weakened by the blows of the ram, and the dislodgment of some of the stones, fell inward of its own accord, with a tremendous crash, spreading alarm through both camp and city. The Romans rushed to arms, and on discovering how matters stood, hastened to the breach to take possession of Antonia, when they were met by the inner wall, which John, foreseeing the possibility of such a disaster had erected behind the first. The courage of the Romans fell at the sight, and the Jews exulted that the fortress was still safe.[2]

The new wall, however, had been hastily constructed, and had not the strength of the first; and besides, the ruins of the outer fortification, which had fallen, much facilitated an escalade. Titus therefore called together his troops, and proclaimed high rewards to those who should first mount the rampart. Sabinus, a Syrian by birth, started from the ranks and offered to lead a forlorn hope, and eleven others volunteered to accompany him. In broad daylight, at 12 at noon, on 30th June,[3] Sabinus and his brave comrades, with their shields over their heads, rushed up the piles of rubbish to the wall. Many were struck down by the missiles from above, but Sabinus and three others gained the summit, and Sabinus waved his sword in triumph. He was dashing against the enemy, when his foot

---

[1] 6.1.3
[2] 6.1.4
[3] 6.1.6

caught a stone, and he tumbled headlong. The Jews turned and threw themselves upon him and prevented his rising. Sabinus, resting upon one knee, fought gallantly against a host of enemies, but, pierced by a hundred wounds, he at last dropped dead at their feet. The three of his comrades who had scaled the wall were also slain, and the other eight were carried off severely wounded.[1]

Two days after this, on 2nd July, occurred one of those strange adventures that serve to diversify the monotony of regular warfare. A strong corps kept watch and ward every night over the Roman works. Twenty of these, without any communication with the commanding officer, concerted a surprise upon the enemy, and enlisted with them the standard-bearer of the 5th Legion, with two cavaliers, and (what proved the most important accession of all) a trumpeter. At 3 o'clock in the morning, when all was still as death, they crept softly up to the wall, found the sentinels asleep, and killed them on the spot, and then the trumpeter sounded a charge. The Jews, imagining that the whole army were upon the wall, gave way to a panic, and fled from Antonia into the Temple. Titus, roused by the din, started to his feet and hurried with his guards to the spot, and on ascertaining the true state of things, poured his troops into Antonia, partly over the wall and partly through the mine which had been excavated by John. Emboldened by their success, the Romans even pursued the Jews along the two cloisters that connected the fortress with the Temple, and tried to force their way within the precincts of the outer court. Here, however, a fierce conflict ensued, the Romans pressing on to consummate their victory by the capture of the Temple, and the Jews feeling that if they lost their Temple they had nothing left worth fighting for. In this emergency, the hardy bands of Simon joined themselves to those of John, and both engaged furiously with the enemy. Javelins and arrows were useless, and it was now a hand-to-hand combat at close quarters. The Romans would fain have given way before the desperate valour of the Jews, but the front ranks, being kept in their places, or even forced forward by the pressure from behind, were obliged to fight, though anxious to fly. The living mass swayed backward and forward, as first one party prevailed and then the other, and the shouts of triumph were mingled with the groans of the dying. Some were

---

[1] 6.1.6

slain, others trodden to death, and the outer court was strewn with dead bodies. The obstinacy of the Jews carried the day, and at 1 o'clock, after ten hours continuous conflict, the Romans, despairing of success, were seen to fall back.[1]

At this moment Julian, a centurion of the Bithynian corps, a distinguished officer, and the bravest of the brave, who happened at the time to be standing near Titus, sprang forward, and forcing his way to the front rank, renewed the fight. The Romans, amazed at the man's gallantry, took him for Castor or Pollux come as of old to the rescue; and the Jews, deeming him more than human, were again driven back across the outer court to the very wall of the Inner Temple. Julian was pressing forward triumphantly, when his nailed shoes slipped on the polished pavement of the outer court, and he was laid on his back. At the clash of his armour the Jews turned and sprang upon their victim. He contracted his neck so as to bring his helmet and breastplate together, and for a long time the Jews could not touch a vital part, while they shockingly mutilated the lower members of his body. Julian, unable to rise, plied his sword, as he lay, with effect against his assailants; but, overpowered by numbers, he at last surrendered his brave spirit, at a costly price to the victors. Titus was looking on at the prodigious exertions of his gallant centurion, and an involuntary cry escaped him as he marked his fall. Now that their champion was dead, the Romans once more lost heart, and were driven inch by inch before the fierce bands of Simon and John, until not a Roman was left in the court of the Temple, and the gates were closed. Titus, however, was left in possession of fort Antonia;[2] and so ended the third act of this bloody drama.

---

[1] 6.1.7
[2] 6.1.8

Chapter 4

'And as some spake of the Temple, how it was adorned with goodly stones and gifts, he said, "As for these things which ye behold, the days will come in the which there shall not be left one stone upon another that shall not be thrown down'—Luke 21:5.

To master the Temple, the next step, was no ordinary task, for though devoted to sacred purposes, it was also a citadel of unusual strength. We have already described the platform on which both it and Antonia stood as about 1,500 feet long from north to south, and 900 feet wide from east to west. The Temple was situated at the south-west corner. The outer court was a square of 600 feet every way, and encompassed by a wall 12 feet thick, and round the three sides of the interior, viz., on the north, east, and west, ran a cloister 45 feet wide, and along the southern side was a triple cloister, 105 feet wide The flat roof of these cloisters served as an admirable post for the movement of troops, and for the disposition of engines of war. Within the outer court was another inner court of rectangular shape (being longer from east to west than it was broad from north to south), and this formed a keep still more formidable. It was ascended on the north, east, and south sides by fourteen steps, but on the west side was a sheer wall of the same height. On the platform at the top of the steps was a wall, 37 1/2 feet high and 12 feet broad, running round the whole, and having cloisters on the interior. This upper platform was divided into two parts. The eastern half was the court of the women, so called from the admission of the women as well as the men thus far, but no farther. The western half contained the altar and Temple, the altar standing on the east, and to the west of it the sacred fabric, consisting of a vestibule to the east, and behind it, on the west, the Holy of Holies. Round the vestibule and Holy of Holies were ranged small chambers in several stories, in which were kept the habiliments of the priests and the stores for the services of the Temple. The upper platform had nine gates—viz., four on the north, and four on the south; and on the east one only, but which, from its magnificence, eclipsed all the rest, being the Corinthian or Beautiful Gate. Of the gates on the north, three of them led up to the court in which were the Temple and altar, and the fourth to the court of the women. The four gates on the south were opposite to them. Had it not been for these nine gates, which presented comparatively weak points, the upper platform might have been regarded as impregnable.[1]

Antonia, now in the possession of the Romans, lay on the north of the Temple, but was not far from it, being removed from it about an interval of 300 feet. It had been originally built as a kind of vestry, for the safe custody of the pontifical robes, and called the Bireh, or in its Greek form, the Baris, or Castle. Herod still farther strengthened and beautified the Baris, and called it, after the name of his friend Mark Antony, Antonia. As left by Herod, it was a quadrangular fortress, about 300 feet on each side; and while, from its regular shape, it presented the appearance, as a whole, of one vast tower, it had also, at each corner, a separate tower rising above the general height, and in particular, at the south-east corner, was a grand tower much exceeding the rest, and attaining an altitude of 105 feet The object of this extra height was that it might command a view of the proceedings in the Temple. As the sacred edifice was the heart of Jerusalem, from which all its pulsations issued, Herod's object was to place it under military control, and this was effected by uniting Antonia to the Temple by means of two connecting cloisters or colonnades parallel to each other. One of them ran from the south-west corner of Antonia to the northwest corner of the Temple, and joined on to the western cloister. The other parallel cloister started from the south-east corner of Antonia, and ran to a point in the northern cloister of the Temple, about 475 feet from the western end, and 125 feet from the eastern end. Thus the troops quartered in the fortress had free access along the two parallel colonnades to the cloisters of the Temple, either along the flat roofs, or along the galleries below. The spirit of the Jews was so disorderly and turbulent, that at every festival, as a matter of course, a cohort was posted on the roof of the western cloister of the Temple to repress the disturbances that were almost sure to occur.

Such were the relative positions of Antonia and the Temple, and Titus being master of the former, had now to concert his measures for the capture of the latter. His first aim was to clear the ground for

---

[1] 5.5.2

the free movement of the troops, and the whole fortress of Antonia was razed and levelled with the exception, first, of the great south-east tower, which would be convenient for watching the enemy, and secondly, of the two parallel cloisters, which would facilitate the assault upon the Temple. The clearance of the ground occupied a space of seven days.[1]

On the 14th of July occurred an event which had the effect of greatly depressing the spirits of the Jews. The daily sacrifice, which had hitherto been regularly offered in the Temple, now for the first time, either from want of victims or want of proper ministers, came to an end. Titus received intelligence of the despondency thus caused, and thought it a suitable opportunity for renewing his overtures. He therefore commissioned Josephus to convey a message to John that the Romans desired the preservation of the Temple and the continuance of the sacrifices, and would afford every facility; that if John relied upon the strength and courage of his troops, the Romans would give him a fair field without the walls, but that the sacred edifice ought not to be sacrificed to the obstinacy of its votaries. Josephus also added his own personal remonstrances, in the hope of bringing his countrymen, at this the eleventh hour, to reason. John replied haughtily that Jehovah would take care of his own sanctuary, and bade the Romans defiance.[2]

The appeal of Josephus, however, produced a great effect upon the priests, the order to which he belonged himself, and also upon many of the higher class, so that considerable numbers watched for their opportunity and escaped to the Romans. Titus, who was near at hand, and could protect them from the violence of the soldiery, received them even with courtesy, and sent them to a distance at Gophna, with a promise that when the war was over he would even restore their possessions.[3]

This act of generosity was intended as a political encouragement to desertion, but such was the subtle and serpent-like astuteness of John, that it was turned to the very opposite account. As the deserters were not to be seen, John spread the rumor that they had been murdered secretly, and hence the feeling that starvation within was

---

[1] 6.2.7
[2] 6.2.1
[3] 6.2.2

preferable to assassination without. When this reached the ears of Titus, he summoned all the deserters from Gophna, and paraded them before the walls, and Josephus again, with tears and entreaties, implored his countrymen to accept the proffered boon. The insurgents were steeled against every argument, and only vented curses against Josephus, whom they branded as a traitor.[1]

As remonstrances were unavailing, Titus had no alternative but an appeal to arms. As he had captured Antonia by a surprise at night, why not the Temple in the same way? Hope whispered the affirmative, and he resolved on the attempt. The space was so confined that only a small portion of his force could act at once, and he therefore selected thirty of the bravest from each century, and placed the whole under the orders of one of his best officers, Sextus Cerealis, the commander of the 5th Legion. Titus was anxious to lead them himself, but it was justly represented that so valuable a life ought not to be lightly committed to the casualties of a sanguinary conflict, and that he would contribute much more to the chances of success by posting himself on the remaining great tower of Antonia, whence he might overlook the exertions of his faithful legionaries, and be enabled to judge of their claims to reward.

The most favorable time for the assault was thought to be three o'clock in the morning, and at that hour Cerealis and his chosen band advanced with as much secrecy and silence as possible along the galleries of the two connecting cloisters to the gates of the outer court below, and along the flat roofs of the connecting cloisters above. Whether it was that the Jews had received intimation of the intended attack, or that from the loss of Antonia they had become more vigilant, they were now on the alert, and the sentries gave the alarm. At once the troops of John rushed to the spot, and were soon followed by those of Simon. A mortal struggle at close quarters commenced, and the dead bodies of Jews and Romans in one blended mass choked the entrances to the Temple. Many of the Jews fell by the hands of their own countrymen, for the followers of Simon and John, having no common watchword, not unfrequently mistook their retreating friends for foes. The day dawned, and still the battle raged. Titus and his staff from Antonia, and John and Simon from the cloisters of the Temple, watched every movement,

---

[1] 6.2.2

and stimulated the ardour of the combatants. The Temple was like a gladiatorial arena, and around were the hosts of spectators, showing by their vociferations and gestures how deeply they participated in every turn of the strife. The onslaught abated not till 11 o'clock in the forenoon, when the dogged courage of the Jews prevailed, and the Romans, beaten back and despairing of success, retired sullenly within the precincts of Antonia, leaving the enemy in possession of the Temple.[1]

It was evident from this failure that any assault without the aid of auxiliary works would be hopeless. Titus therefore ordered the erection of four mounds, two within the site of Antonia, or rather between the two parallel cloisters that connected Antonia with the Temple, and two others on the exterior. Of those *within* Antonia one was opposite the north-west corner of the Inner Temple, and the other opposite the alcove, between the two middle gates of the court of the Inner Temple, which contained the sacred fabric. Of those *without* Antonia, one was directed against the northern cloister of the Outer Temple, and was therefore a little eastward of the eastern parallel which connected Antonia with the Temple, and the other was against the western cloister of the Outer Temple, and opposite the alcove in the west wall of the Inner Temple.[2] These works proceeded but slowly, for, in the first place, the Romans had to bring the materials a greater distance than ever, and when the timber was collected the artisans were annoyed by incessant flights of missiles from those who manned the walls.

The only relief to the monotony of this daily warfare was an attempt of the Jews on one occasion to force the wall of circum-vallation. As the 10th Legion, which was quartered on Mount Olivet, was known to take their principal meal at five o'clock in the afternoon, it was hoped that they might be surprised, and at that hour

---

[1] 6.2.5

[2] 6.2.7; 6.4.1. As the alcove was probably in the middle of the western wall of the Inner Temple, the first wall must have crossed from Sion to the south of this; or the Romans, who had not yet captured the first wall, could not have thrown up this mound. On the other hand, as the first wall joined the western cloister of the Temple, and not the southern, it could not have passed over the bridge which led to the centre nave of the royal or southern cloister. The wall, therefore, must have crossed between these two points, i. e. at the wailing place, where the square holes in the stones seem to indicate the former junction of another building.

a strong band sallied from the eastern gate, rushed up the slope of Olivet, and approached the circumvallation wall. But the Romans had suffered too often before from the adventurous spirit of the Jews to be thus caught off their guard, and, before the insurgents could reach the goal, the alarm was given, and the troops, seizing their arms, ran together to the spot, and presented such a serried front that an ill-organized band, however brave, could have no chance of breaking it. Impetuous and fierce as was the onset of the Jews, it was met by the cool and disciplined courage of the Romans, and, after a short and sharp struggle, the Jews were driven down the hill in confusion, and made for the gate. A trooper in pursuit greatly signalized himself on this occasion by a feat of muscular strength. From his horse's back, and at full tilt, he seized a fugitive, and holding him by the heel, carried him off in triumph, and threw him down at the feet of Titus.[1]

Escape was now more than ever hopeless, and the Jews, having to defend themselves as best they could within the walls, committed an act of desecration that shocked the consciences of the more religious part of the community. The two connecting cloisters that incorporated Antonia with the courts of the Temple were regarded as parts of the sacred edifice, and had hitherto been spared both by Romans and Jews. At the same time, these corridors offered facilities for mutual assaults, and particularly the western parallel had been employed by the Romans as a ready approach against the enemy. The Jews therefore resolved on its destruction, and on the 19th of July they cut away thirty feet of the parallel at its junction to the northern cloister of the Temple, and then set fire to the rest of it. The work of desecration once begun by the Jews, was soon followed up by the Romans, who two days after, on the 21st of July, set fire to the eastern parallel, and, as the flames advanced southward, the Jews, to save the northern cloister of the Temple, were obliged to sever that parallel also from the courts of the Temple by cutting away the point of junction.[2] This greatly dispirited the Jews, for an old prophecy ran:

'When square the walls.

---

[1] 6.2.8
[2] 6.9.4

The Temple falls;'[1]

and now this had come to pass. The Temple had comprised not only the outer court, a regular square of 600 feet, but also Antonia, which was united to the Temple by the connecting parallels, and so gave it an irregular configuration; but now that the parallels were broken away, the Temple was seen to stand an isolated square, and the morbid imaginations of the beholders already pictured the holy fabric enveloped in flames.

The mound against the western cloister was approaching completion, and then the outer court would of course be in the power of the Romans. But apparently there was no need to wait for this, for the western cloister was so ill guarded that with a little spirit it might be stormed. The Jews, as if despairing of defense in that part, seemed to have lost their energy. The troops collected there were few in number, and the engines of war had been removed elsewhere. The golden opportunity was seized, and scaling ladders were brought, and the Romans, running up, mounted upon the cloister. The Jews fled, and the bands of Romans, following in quick succession, covered the spacious roof.

Just as the Romans raised a shout of triumph they found themselves engulfed in a sea of flame. The subtle genius of John had lined the hollow space between the rafters and the ceiling with dry wood, pitch, and bitumen, and at the right moment the whole was set on fire. Great was the consternation of the legionaries on finding themselves thus entrapped. Some were overtaken by the flames, and were smothered or burnt; some, in anticipation, laid violent hands on themselves; some leaped down into the outer court and were dispatched by the Jews; some precipitated themselves on the other side into the city, and were taken up dead or with broken limbs; others, springing from the roof of the cloister upon the wall, ran along it until they were shot down by the Jewish missiles. One Artorius escaped by a singular artifice. Standing on the verge of the wall, he shouted to those below, 'Whoever catches me shall be my heir!' A Roman started forward and accepted the terms. The expectant heir was dashed to the ground and killed; Artorius sur-

---

[1] 6.5.4

vived![1]

Toward the southern end of the western cloister was the bridge, which crossed the valley westward by a succession of arches to the opposite hill, on which stood the High Town. This was the grand approach to the Temple, and, in the wars between John and Simon, John had erected a tower in the western cloister of the Temple, at the eastern end of the bridge, to check incursions by the partisans of Simon, who occupied the High Town. The whole of the western cloister, from the northern termination down to this tower of John, was now destroyed by the fire; and so perished one limb of the magnificent cloisters,[2] erected at so vast an expense by Herod. The western cloister was that on which the Roman cohorts had been wont to station themselves to overawe the tumultuous masses in the court below; and they little dreamt that this, their post of pride, would one day be their grave.

The next day the Romans, who had hitherto endeavored to save the Temple in its integrity, set fire themselves to the northern cloister, and the whole of it from east to west was burnt to the ground. Thus, both on the west and north sides, the Inner Temple was now exposed to the invader, and yet, seated as it was upon a high terrace, surrounded with a strong wall bristling with arms and engines of war, it still frowned defiance.

Dreadful as were the ravages of war, still more appalling, meanwhile, were the fatal effects of the famine. The provisions of the city had been utterly used up, and the insurgents, no longer finding victims for plunder, were at their wits' end to support life. Occasionally, a Roman cavalry horse would stray to the neighborhood of the gates, when a starving band would rush out and capture the beast; but what was this among so many thousands? Even these windfalls were soon cut off, for Titus, justly imputing the loss of their horses to the negligence of the riders, ordered a soldier who had suffered in this way to instant execution, and this act of severity had the desired effect of preventing the recurrence of the complaint.[3] The besieged now staggered about from weakness, like

---

[1] 6.3.1

[2] Covered walkways, usually a sequence of arches, with a flat roof. They are most often found today in monastaries.

[3] 6.2.7

drunken men, and their senses being unhinged and their memory gone, they would break into the same house two or three times the same day in search of food, unconscious that they had paid the like visit before. In the extremity of their distress they gnawed the hides from their shields and the leather of their belts and shoes, and even a wisp of hay or straw was found a relief to the pangs of hunger.[1] But one horrible deed eclipses all the rest:—A lady of rank and fortune, Mary, the daughter of Eleazar, had been obliged to fly from Perea beyond Jordan to take refuge in Jerusalem. The insurgents had stripped her house of every article of food, and left her and her infant child to starve. As the armed brigands passed her door they inhaled the fumes of the kitchen, and rushed into the house, and threatened instant death unless the savoury viands were disclosed. She led them aside and showed them, to their horror, the remains of her child. Maddened by the cravings of nature, she had murdered the infant at her breast and cooked it for food![2]

The bank against the western wall of the Inner Temple had now been carried across the smouldering ruins of the western cloister and the outer court, and the battering-ram mounted upon it was made to play against the Inner Temple in vain, for such was the compactness of the solid mass of masonry that the ram produced no effect. Another more powerful engine was substituted, but no better result followed. For six days the most persevering efforts were continued, and then the Romans gave it up in despair.[3]

Meanwhile, a second bank had also been perfected, viz., the bank outside of Antonia, directed against the northern cloister of the Inner Temple. It had gradually progressed across the debris of the northern cloister of the Outer Temple, which had been burnt, and across the outer court, and now approached the foot of the most easterly of the four northern gates of the Inner Temple. Titus at this time was anxious to save the sacred fabric with its cloisters as a trophy of arms, and ordered his legionaries to force the gate opposite the bank with crowbars and levers, and after great exertions a few of the stones at the threshold were dislodged, but the gate itself, supported by the solid masses at the side and the supports within,

---

[1] 6.3.3
[2] 6.3.4
[3] 6.4.1

stood firm. Titus ordered an escalade, and ladders were brought, and the Romans mounted with alacrity. Indeed, the Jews offered little resistance to the ascent, but no sooner were the Romans up than some were sabred as they stepped off the ladders; others, who had gained a footing on the wall, were surrounded and slain, and not a few of the ladders, loaded with men, were thrown backward, and all upon it dashed headlong against the hard pavement below. Titus did not yet despair, but ordered up the colors, or ensigns, in the hope that his legionaries would at least rally round these. The Jews even allowed the standards to be carried up upon the wall, but there ensued a deadly and desperate conflict between the Romans in defense of their colors, and the Jews to get possession of them. The Jews again prevailed, and bore off the colors in triumph. This indelible disgrace to the Roman arms was witnessed by the assembled force below, but not a man who had mounted the cloister ever rejoined the ranks.[1]

The battery from the western mound had failed, and the attempt to force the northern gate had failed, and the escalade had failed, and Titus, disappointed and nettled, commanded his troops to set fire to the magnificent gate which had thus successfully resisted his efforts. The soldiery were but too ready to obey the behest, and in a minute the northern gate was in a blaze. The plates of silver that covered it flowed down in liquid streams, and, as might or must have been foreseen, the gorgeous cloisters that communicated with it became also the prey of the devouring element. Now it was that the spirit of the Jews for the moment was broken; stricken to the earth by consternation at the depth of the calamity, they became paralysed, and made no effort to extinguish the flames, but looked on in silent despair. This was on the 3rd of August, and for the rest of the day and throughout the night the conflagration continued.[2]

On the 4th of August, the sacred fabric, though encircled by flames, was still standing, and Titus called a council of his generals to deliberate upon its fate. Besides Titus, there were present the six most prominent personages of the army, viz., Tiberius Alexander, the second in command; Sextus Cerealis, the commander of the 5th Legion; Larcius Lapidus of the 10th; Titus Phrygius of the 15th;

---

[1] 6.4.1
[2] 6.4.2

Fronto of Liternum, who led the Alexandrian cohorts; and Marcus Antonius Julianus, the Procurator of Judaea. Some cried impetuously, 'Down with the Temple to the ground!' for that it was the very heart and centre of the whole rebellion. Others advised more guardedly, that if abandoned by the Jews it should be preserved, but if converted into a citadel or military position, it ought to be razed. Titus expressed his opinion that the sanctuary, whatever use might be made of it by the Jews, ought, for their own sake, to be saved as a monument of their prowess. Alexander, Cerealis, and Fronto expressed their concurrence in this view, and the majority therefore favored the preservation of the Temple. Orders were given for preventing the conflagration from reaching the sanctuary, and to clear the ground for an assault upon the platform on which it stood. The Romans were occupied the rest of the day upon these works, and the Jews, dejected by the destruction of the cloister, did not venture upon a renewal of hostilities.[1]

The 5th of August, a day of ominous import, dawned upon the besieged. It was on that very day that the Temple of Solomon had been burnt by Nebuchadnezzar. Was the Temple of Herod to share the same fate on the same day? The partisans of John and Simon showed no superstitious dread of it, for their courage, which had slumbered all the day before, now rose to its highest pitch, and at eight o'clock in the morning, sallying from the eastern gate, they rushed down upon the Roman legionaries. The Romans formed in close rank, and, armed with large shields, stood like a wall to receive their charge, but the Jews poured down in ever-increasing numbers, and would have prevailed had not Titus, who was on the look-out from the remaining tower of Antonia, hastened with his chosen guard to their relief. Narrow as the space was, it is said that even a body of cavalry rode in amongst the Jews, and trampled them down. The contest was a severe one, and it was not till one o'clock in the day that the Jews, exhausted and overmatched, were driven back, and again shut up within the walls of the Inner Temple.[2]

Titus having secured the victory to his troops, retired to his tent to repose himself after his fatigues. The troops proceeded to clear the ground, and the enemy offering no resistance, they ascended the

---

[1] 6.4.8
[2] 6.14.4

platform to extinguish the smoldering fires of the cloisters. All at once the indomitable bands of John and Simon, having recovered breath after the morning's exertion, rushed upon their foes and engaged in another death struggle. At this moment a soldier, without orders, and actuated only by the spirit of revenge, seized a burning brand from the cloister, and mounting on the back of a comrade, hurled it into the window of one of the side chambers that enclosed the sacred fabric on the north. Ignition in the hot month of August was easy, and in a few minutes the flames were seen to ascend. A convulsive cry arose from the Jews as they beheld their beloved Temple approaching its fate. They sprang to the rescue, but extinguishment was beyond human effort.[1]

Tidings came to Titus in his tent that the Temple was on fire, and he instantly started up, and, accompanied by his body-guard of spearmen, commanded by Liberatus, hastened to the spot. All the officers followed in his wake, and after them the legionaries *en masse*. Titus forced his way into the first court of the Inner Temple, the court of the women, and then into the second court, which contained the sacred fabric, and by shouts and gestures implored the assembled multitudes to assist in subduing the flames, but the clamor and din that reigned on all sides drowned his voice, and distracted attention from his gestures. The confusion was increased by the legionaries, who had climbed the ascent after him in a tumultuous body. The entrances to the upper platform were choked with men, and some fell and were trampled to death, and others were thrown down amongst the smoldering ruins of the cloister, and suffocated or burnt. Those who reached the sanctuary paid not the least regard to the commands or remonstrances, or even the threats of Titus, but, instead of averting destruction from the holy pile, encouraged those before them to complete its destruction.[2]

Titus saw that the fate of the Temple was sealed, and eager, from natural curiosity, to inspect the interior of perhaps the most celebrated edifice in the world, he hastened with his guards to the vestibule, and entered the Holy or first shrine, and then the Holy of Holies. The flames had hitherto enveloped the chambers only round the exterior, and had not touched the sanctuary itself, and Titus was

---

[1] 6.4.5
[2] 6.4.6

so struck with the beauty and magnificence of what he beheld, that the thought still recurred, was it not possible to save this glorious production of human skill? He rushed back through the portal, and again implored the Romans to exert themselves to preserve so renowned a monument, and even ordered Liberatus, the centurion of his guard, to inflict corporal chastisement on any that disobeyed. All was in vain. The fury of the soldiery predominated, and even his own immediate followers were so far from paying respect to his injunctions, that one of them, as Titus left the sanctuary, thrust a burning flambeau into the woodwork of the doorway, and the whole Temple now became one volume of fire. Seated as it was upon an elevated platform, it presented the appearance of a vast volcano surging and seething from the bowels of the earth, and vomiting a sea of flame up to the skies.

The roar of the conflagration was only equaled by the shouts of the triumphant Romans and the shrieks of their despairing victims. The whole upper city, though divided by a valley, was a spectator of this scene of devastation, and the hills around re-echoed a nation's wail.[1]

What became of the desperate bands of John and Simon? Driven by fire and sword from the fastness of the Inner Temple, they lost not their wonted energy, but facing the dense ranks of the legionaries that surrounded them, cut their way through to the outer court, and thence gained the bridge that led from the southwest corner of the outer court, and reached in safety the Upper Town to bid defiance once more to the Roman arms.[2]

The scene that they left behind them beggars all description. A general carnage, remorseless and indiscriminate, followed, and men unarmed and begging on their knees for mercy, priests in their robes, women and children, were murdered in the madness of the moment, without regard to the laws of war, without distinction of age, or sex, or office. Streams of blood were seen to flow down the steps of the altar, and the pavement was covered with dead bodies, over which the brutal soldiery still struggled in pursuit of the wretched fugitives.[3]

---

[1] 6.4.7
[2] 6.5.1
[3] 6.5.1

Some anticipated death from the hand of the enemy by precipitating themselves into the flames. A numerous body of the priests found their way to the top of the broad wall of the Inner Temple, and there stood motionless as statues aghast at the sight before them. A multitude of the populace, amounting to 6,000, took refuge on the roof of the royal cloister, along the south side of the Outer Temple. The Romans most inhumanly set fire to the latter cloister, and not a living soul of all the 6,000 escaped. As for the priests who still survived upon the wall of the Inner Temple, they were soon driven by famine to surrender at discretion, and Titus ordered them all to execution, with the cold remark that, as the Temple was destroyed, their office was gone, and that the priests of the Temple who had lived by it should also perish with it.

The Romans even wreaked their vengeance upon inanimate objects; for, leaving only the bare walls of the Inner Temple, they destroyed what remained of the cloisters, and demolished the gates with the exception of the Beautiful Gate on the east, and the Royal Gate on the south, which were for the present spared. They also delivered over to the flames the famous Treasury, in which, as the great national bank, vast heaps of wealth had been accumulated.[1]

The Romans now in triumph carried their ensigns into the Temple, and, planting them opposite the Beautiful or Corinthian Gate (the eastern), offered sacrifices to them, according to their custom, and saluted Titus as Imperator.[2] Thus stood, in the Holy Place, the abomination of desolation spoken of by the prophet Daniel, and so dropped the curtain upon the fourth act of this mournful tragedy.

---

[1] 6.5.2
[2] 6.6.1

Chapter 5

'They shall fall by the edge of the sword, and shall be led away captive into all nations: and Jerusalem shall be trodden down of the Gentiles, until the times of the Gentiles be fulfilled.'—Luke 21:24.

TITUS had mastered successively the New Town or Cenopolis, and the Inner Low Town, a part of Acra, and the Temple Platform, another part of Acra; and by the possession of the Temple Platform he held the key of the Outer Low Town, the remaining part of Acra, situated on Ophel to the south of the Temple. The Outer Low Town had no independent defenses on the north, and could therefore at any time be deluged by troops from the Temple. The only quarter of the city that could still maintain itself was the High Town or Upper Market, now called Sion, which, being surrounded by valleys, and surmounted besides by a strong wall, could bid defiance for a time to any assault.

The united bands of Simon and John, who held the High Town, had been much weakened by desertion, and still more by the inroads of famine, and could not hope to resist the regular approaches of the Roman arms for any lengthened period. Simon and John therefore invited Titus to a parley, and Titus, having no thirst for blood, except as means to an end, acceded to the request. The place fixed upon for the interview, had it been designed for the purpose, could not have been more favorable. It was the great bridge or viaduct, 51 feet wide (for the base of one of the arches still remains), which led from the royal cloister, at the south-west corner of the Temple, across the Tyropoeon valley to the opposite hill. At the eastern end it was flanked on the north side by the tower which John had erected against the incursions of Simon, and at the western end it was flanked on the south side by the tower which Simon had erected against the incursions of John. Titus, with an interpreter, and surrounded by his guard, took his stand at the eastern end of the bridge, and Simon and John, with their adherents, at the western end.[1]

Titus, as the superior, opened the conference, and expostulated

---

[1] 6.6.2

with the Jews on the obstinacy which had already led to the destruction of the Temple and the greater part of the city—that all the
world, nay, the Britons, who were outside the world, had done
homage to the Romans; and Titus ended by offering them their lives
if the insurgents would lay down their arms and surrender themselves prisoners of war.

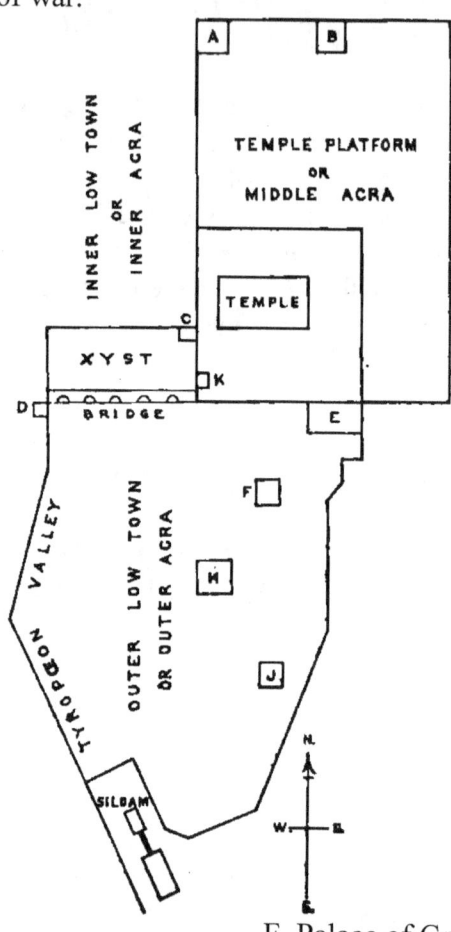

A. The Acra.

B. The Archive.

C. The Council-house.

D. The Tower of Simon.

E. Ophla.

F. Palace of Grapte.

H. Palace of Helena.

J. Palace of Monobazus.

K. Tower of John.

Simon and John replied that they and their adherents had bound
themselves, by a solemn oath to Almighty God, never to surrender

themselves into the hands of the Romans; but they expressed their willingness to retire with their wives and children into the wilderness, and leave the Romans in possession of the city. Titus considered this language, from men in their desperate condition, as a mockery, and answered sternly that henceforth he would receive no deserters and show no mercy, and they might fight their hardest.[1]

Nothing more was done on that day, but on the following the work of desolation began by the destruction of the remaining public buildings about the Temple Platform.

The first prey to the flames was the Archive, situated in the middle of the northern wall of the Temple Platform, and, in the time of the kings of Judah, used as the King's Bench, or royal seat for the administration of justice. Annexed to it were the prison and stocks in which the Prophet Jeremiah had been confined by King Zedekiah. Fire was next applied to the Acra, at the north-west corner of the Temple Platform, and so called from its occupying the site of the famous Acra of the Macedonians. The latter had been razed, and the rock on which it stood had been cut away, but a wall of rock had been left and a tower erected for the defense of the Platform, in the place of the Acra. Next was consumed the Council-house, half-way down the west side of the Temple Platform, in which, during the domination of the Romans, the Sanhedrim had been wont to hold its sittings. It stood on or near the spot where is still the Mekhimeh, or Town-hall. The fatal brand next invaded Ophla, the inclosure on the south of the Temple platform, occupied by the priests and servants of the Temple, and from Ophla the flames spread southward, consuming whole streets, as far as the Palace of Helena, Queen of Adiabene.[2] Many of the houses were in truth funeral piles, for they were filled with dead bodies which the survivors had not possessed the strength to carry out of the walls, but had stowed away in these charnel-houses. In the times of David and Solomon, Ophel (for so the wedge-like hill on the south of the Platform is called) had been the seat of royalty, but Herod had transferred his palace to the north-west corner of the High Town. However, Ophel was still distinguished as the residence of the royal family of Adiabene. In the middle of Ophel stood the noble Palace of Helena, a spacious

---

[1] 6.6.3
[2] 6.6.3

building, and of great strength, and at this time the repository not only of the Adiabene treasures, but also of the valuable effects of the other inhabitants of the Outer Low Town. Near it had been erected a palace by Grapte, another member of the same family, and more to the south another palace still by Monobazus, the brother of Izates, and son of Helena. Hitherto the descendants of Helena, whether from necessity or choice, had taken an active part with the insurgents against the Romans, but now that the conflagration approached the Palace of Helena, where all their wealth was hoarded, their hearts failed them, and they went over in a body to the Romans. Titus had declared that henceforth no deserters would be received, but royal blood pleaded powerfully, and their lives were spared. They were not set at liberty, however, but were reserved as hostages for the good behaviour of their countrymen.[1]

No sooner was the tergiversation of the Adiabene clan discovered by the insurgents than, urged by a spirit of vengeance as well as of plunder, they rushed to the Palace of Helena and (with the exception of two Romans whom they found there) murdered all who had taken refuge within its walls, amounting to many thousands. Of the two Romans, one was a legionary, and the other a trooper. Revenge is sweet, on however small a scale and however shortlived, and the poor legionary was led to the block. The trooper intimated that he had an important disclosure to make, and was conducted into the presence of Simon; but it was a mere subterfuge, and he also was ordered for execution. As the fatal axe was raised, he, by a convulsive effort, set free his hands, tore the bandage from his eyes, and, darting forward, escaped to the Roman camp. Titus would not take his life, but cashiered him from the army as unworthy after captivity to carry the Roman arms.[2]

The insurgents plundered the Palace of Helena of all its treasures, sacked the rest of the Outer Low Town, and then carried off their booty into the High Town, where they took their stand. Titus, irritated at seeing his prey escape from his hands, ordered what remained of the Outer Low Town to be burnt, and the flames now extended down to the very southern point of the wedge overlooking the fountain of Siloam, so that the hill of Ophel, from the Temple

---

[1] 6.6.4
[2] 6.7.1

Platform to Siloam, became one scene of desolation.[1] At the present day, if it were not for the occasional escarpment of the rock, and the abundance of pottery that everywhere appears on turning up the soil, no one would imagine that this had once been a beautiful and populous quarter of old Jerusalem.

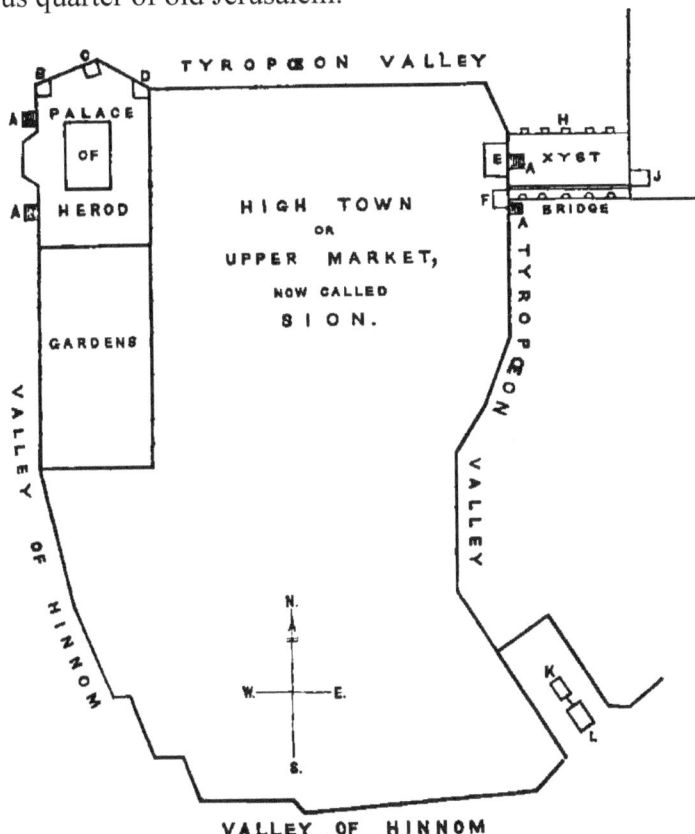

A A A A. The four Mounds or Banks.

B. The tower Hippicus.

C. The tower Phasaelus.

D. The tower Mariamne.

E. The Palace of Agrippa.

F. The tower of Simon.

H. Wall from High Town to the Temple.

J. The tower of John.

K. The Pool of Siloam.

L. The King's Pool.

As the High Town was defended by ravines—namely, the valley of Hinnom on the south and west, and the Tyropoeon on the east and

---

[1] 6.7.2

north—and was also fortified by a wall, it was necessary to proceed against it by regular approaches; and on the 15th of August directions were given for the erection of banks, some on the west side of the city against the Palace of Herod, and others on the east side, in the neighbourhood of the Temple. The army was divided into two bodies, one the legionary force, and the other the allies. To the four legions were assigned the banks on the west, and to the allies the banks on the east. It is remarkable that on this occasion only is mention made of the allies as taking an active part in the siege.

We know from incidental notices that Agrippa, King of Trachonitis, Antiochus from Commagene, and the King of Petra, either personally or by deputy, and no doubt several others, were present with their respective contingents, and from this distribution of the banks by Titus between the legions on the west and the allies on the east, one is led to suppose, as probably was the fact, that the allies were almost, if not altogether, as numerous as the Romans; and yet the courtly Josephus, from his strong leaning in favor of Vespasian and Titus, to whose protection and patronage he owed his life and fortune, gives no credit for any exploit to the allies, but attributes the success of the siege throughout solely and exclusively to the Romans. It must be confessed that while in general, and where not warped by personal interest, Josephus is an accurate and faithful historian, yet where his narrative concerns the Romans on the one hand, and the Jewish factions opposed to Josephus personally on the other, his impartiality is open to suspicion. Had any of the adherents of Simon or John written an account of the siege, we might have looked upon a very different picture. Josephus presents Simon and John to us in colors calculated only to excite abhorrence; but the steady and unflinching courage with which to the last, and even against hope, they maintained their independence against the overwhelming numbers of the enemy (a struggle that has scarcely a counterpart in history), prompts the thought that, after all, they glowed with the noble fire of patriotism, and were actuated by higher and more creditable motives than any assigned to them by the Roman-Jewish historian.

The point selected for the banks on the west was one which was *naturally* the weakest, but *artificially* the strongest. At the north-west corner of the High Town, the valley of Hinnom coming up from the south, and here comparatively shallow, shoots off in a northwestern direction, and, on the other hand, the Tyropoeon valley ascending from the east, and running along the foot of the north wall of the High Town, is, at its termination at the north-west corner, almost on a level with the adjacent ground. Thus the High Town may be regarded as a peninsula hanging to the mainland by an isthmus at the north-west corner. Fortunately, just where the neck of the isthmus begins rises a rocky knoll, and from the earliest times this has been occupied by works of the greatest strength. It was the citadel erected on this spot that induced the Jebusites of old to throw out the taunt against David that 'the blind and the lame could keep the ramparts.' In the days of Herod the royal palace was transferred to this angle of the High Town, and was fortified by a wall of amazing strength on the west, and by the three famous towers, Hippicus, Phasaelus, and Mariamne, on the north. As the palace with its outworks commanded the High Town, which could not be held by an enemy without possession of the castle, the object now was to storm it by banks, and all the four legions were employed upon the task.[1]

The banks committed to the allies on the east of the High Town were constructed by them opposite the Temple, where the brow of the High Town at the north-east corner is considerably depressed below the height which it attains a little more to the south. From the south-west corner of the Temple ran, as we have said, a bridge of great breadth, and consisting of several successive arches, across the Tyropoeon valley to the High Town. On the north of the bridge, and between it and a junction wall which connected the wall of the High Town with the Temple, lay the Xyst or Gymnasium; and on the south of the bridge, at the western end, was the tower erected by Simon against the incursions of John. The mounds of the allies rested on the Xyst and on the bridge itself, and were also over against the tower of Simon. The Palace of Herod Agrippa (distinct from the Palace of Herod the Great) was at the end of the bridge, and overlooked the Xyst, so that Agrippa with his forces was engaged in erecting a bank against his own palace.[2]

Within the city it was evident that the end was drawing nigh.

---

[1] 6.8.1
[2] 6.8.1

Simon and John, faithful to their oaths, maintained their equanimity, but the ranks of their followers showed from day to day a marked diminution. A main part of the forces of Simon consisted of a body of Idumeans who had originally attached themselves to John. The Idumeans, while they regarded Jerusalem as the metropolis of the Jewish stock to which they claimed affinity, had not the same warmth of feeling towards it that animated its genuine and native inhabitants. The valour and tact of Simon had hitherto retained them in allegiance, but now, aghast, at the Gorgon features of approaching death, they entered upon a secret conspiracy to abandon so hopeless a cause and tender submission to the Romans. Five of the most influential amongst them were commissioned to negotiate, and they succeeded in opening a communication with the enemy's camp. Titus, notwithstanding his previous denunciations, was not indisposed to listen to their overtures; for, if the Idumeans could be detached from Simon, his remaining adherents would fall an easy prey. Simon, however, as watchful as he was brave, was made acquainted with the plan before it could be executed, and acted with his wonted energy. The five negotiators were seized and executed on the spot. The officers of the Idumeans were put under arrest and imprisoned; and the Idumeans themselves, though allowed to retain their arms, were not employed in manning the walls, or at any post where fidelity would be exposed to temptation.[1]

The utmost circumspection was exercised by Simon and John to prevent desertion, and at night their followers who could be relied upon were wont to ensconce themselves amongst the ruins without the walls, to intercept fugitives and slay them on the spot. But, notwithstanding every precaution, defection still continued and increased. The only alternatives open to the besieged were to die of the famine within, or to hazard death without—first, from the insurgents who lay in ambush to intercept them; and, secondly, from the hands of the Romans. The latter danger, however, was daily diminishing; for the Romans, weary of so many executions, found it much easier and more profitable to sell the able-bodied as slaves, and send the refuse about their business to perish on the mountains. Such was the glut of the slave-market, that even the most eligible lots commanded little more than nominal prices. The unhappy cit-

---

[1] 6.8.2

izens who could not effect their escape from the walls, staggered about the streets until they could stand no longer, and then sank down, with hollow cheeks and attenuated bodies, to wait for the release of death. At this time there was not a spot within the city that was not tainted by the presence of a putrefying corpse.[1]

The progress of the Roman banks was slow, for materials were scarce, and piles and planks in abundance were necessary for giving consistency to the causeways on which the battering-rams were to be worked. At length, on the 1st of September, after eighteen days' incessant labor, the banks on the west against Herod's Palace were completed, and the engines of war brought to bear upon the western wall.[2] Feeble was the opposition offered, for, while the most valiant of the insurgents remained at their post, others fled, for greater safety, to the three towers, Hippicus, Phasaelus, and Mariamne; and others, more alarmed still, hid themselves in the caverns. On the 2nd of September the battering-ram accomplished its work, and a long line of the western wall fell to the ground. General consternation, even before the Romans had mounted the breach, invaded the city. Simon and John were first for cutting their way out through the ranks of the enemy, or dying in the attempt; but when they looked around them, and saw the paucity of their followers, they felt the madness of such an experiment. Two alternatives remained—either to occupy the three great towers, and fight from them to the last, or, issuing through the southern gate, to try and force the wall of cir-cumvallation. There was little time for reflection, for tidings came pouring in that the whole western wall was down—that the Romans had entered the city—that they were carrying all before them, and were searching for the insurgent leaders. Happily for the besiegers, but injudiciously for the besieged, Simon and John resolved on abandoning the towers, and throwing all their remaining force against the wall of circumvallation on the south. They rushed down to Siloam, and attempted to storm the wall. The besieged were for the moment the besiegers, but they had no engines of war, and were, besides, few in number, and enfeebled by famine. They would fain have scaled the wall, but the Romans ran together from all sides, and overmatched the insurgents in numbers, and drove them back in

---

[1] 6.8.2
[2] 6.8.4

dismay. They were now like timid hares surrounded by the net of the hunter, and fled back to the city, and dispersed themselves in different directions.[1]

The Romans, during the interim, had entered the breach, and mounted the wall in triumph, clapping their hands, and singing the paean of victory. They then advanced to the three great towers, and found them deserted. Titus stood amazed at their strength and solidity, and exclaimed that God indeed was on their side, for by man alone these impenetrable masses could not have been taken.[2] The Romans next spread themselves through the streets, slaying all who came in their way, without distinction of age or sex, and sacking and burning the houses. They were however but little prepared for some of the sights of horror that now greeted them. They broke open mansions, for instance, and found them charnel-houses, frill of putrefying corpses. In other houses were seen whole families and their domestics lying dead in the different apartments, the victims of the famine. All that day the butchery and depredation continued, and at night the flaming houses afforded a more appalling spectacle still, from the contrast of the surrounding darkness.[3]

The next day Titus issued a general order that only such as were found in arms should be slain, and that all others should be taken prisoners; but such an order was more easily published than executed, and the infuriate soldiery still continued the slaughter of all who could not be turned to profit as slaves. Such as were in the prime of life, and would fetch a price in the market, were shut up for the present within the charred walls of the Court of the Women, the more easterly court of the Inner Temple, and were placed under the surveillance of one of Titus's freedmen. No less than 11,000 of them are said to have there perished from want of food and air. Of the survivors some were selected to grace the triumphal procession at Rome, and of the remainder all under the age of seventeen were sold as slaves, and all above that age were, a part of them, distributed amongst the theatres of Syria, to fight as gladiators or with wild beasts, and the rest of them condemned for the remainder of their

---

[1] 6.8.4
[2] 6.9.1
[3] 6.8.5

lives to the public works in Egypt.[1]

No more victims for slaughter or plunder were visible above ground; but the Romans were resolved not to leave their work incomplete, and applied themselves to the discovery of such as had buried themselves under ground in the holes and caverns.

Every house in Jerusalem had a cistern under it, and the whole city was underlaid with conduits, sewers, and secret passages, and in these dark recesses multitudes of miserable fugitives had sought a refuge from the storm.[2] To see the victors armed with spade and pickaxe, delving into the bowels of the earth, one would have supposed that they were seeking to unearth some noxious vermin rather than searching for their fellow-men. The mere thirst for blood could not have furnished a sufficient stimulant, but to this was added the passion for gold. The wealth of Judaea had been collected into Jerusalem, and it was the prevalent belief that vast treasures had been carried off by those who escaped. The Romans had no plan of nether Jerusalem as they had of the streets above, and they prosecuted a rigorous search into these subterranean vaults. Some of them were filled with dead bodies; in others the dead and the living were mingled together promiscuously, and not a few even of the victors lost their lives in searching amongst the putrefying bodies. The fugitives that were found alive were put to death, for it was less trouble to kill at once than to take charge of them as prisoners.[3]

All the population of Jerusalem had been either slain or made captive, and orders were now given that (with the exception of two or three memorials) the whole city should be razed to the ground, that every vestige of it might be obliterated from the face of the earth. The western wall of Herod's Palace, at the north-west corner of Sion, had attached to it extensive barracks; and, as Titus purposed to quarter one of his legions for a time at Jerusalem, it was thought prudent to leave this part standing for their accommodation. The three famous towers, also, of Hippicus, Phasaelus, and Mariamne, would show, from their immense strength, against what mighty obstacles the Romans had contended, and were therefore spared. But, with these exceptions, walls, palaces, and mansions were con-

---

[1] 6.9.2
[2] 6.9.4
[3] 6.9.4

signed to one universal ruin. The scant remnants of the Temple that still remained were utterly subverted, so that neither wall, nor cloister, nor altar, nor building of any kind, could any longer be distinguished.[1] So literally and signally was fulfilled the prediction of our Lord uttered thirty-seven years before, that of the Temple 'there should not be left one stone upon another that should not be thrown down.' The whole city was thus made one vast heap, and 'the joy of the whole earth' became a blasted wilderness. Thus ended the fifth and last act of that bloody tragedy, the Siege of Jerusalem.

*****

What had become of Simon Bar-Gioras and John of Gischala, who had played so conspicuous a part in the defense of the city? When the last wall was captured, and the deluge of the Roman army rushed in, Simon and John were nowhere to be found. They were not amongst the living, and their bodies were not recognised amongst the dead. It was some days after the final capture that, as the Roman sentries paced backward and forward, and kept watch and ward, an emaciated figure, with haggard looks and dishevelled hair, rose from the ground, and proclaimed himself to be John of Gischala. He had lowered himself, with a stock of provisions, into one of the secret passages, and now from pressure of hunger was constrained to deliver himself up into the hands of the Romans. He was conducted into the presence of Titus, and ordered to be kept in chains for exhibition to the Roman public at the triumph of Titus.[2] Simon Bar-Gioras was still missing, and his fate was not known until many days, if not weeks, subsequently.

Titus now took upon himself the pleasing duty of recompensing his soldiers by the distribution of rewards. A high platform was erected in the middle of his camp—not that within the third or outer wall, which was of comparatively small dimensions,[3] but that without the wall to the north of Psephinus, where Titus on first investing the city had pitched his tent with the 12th and 15th Legions. Titus ascended the lofty tribune, and the martial host were gathered around him. He thanked them for their steady obedience to orders

---

[1] 7.1.1
[2] 6.9.4
[3] See illustration in chapter 2

and courage on the field, qualities which combined had brought about such glorious results. He admired and loved them; for their loyal and gallant bearing, and, while all were meritorious, many, favored by fortune, had entitled themselves to a special distinction. A list was then read aloud of such as had displayed extraordinary gallantry, and as the names were called over, Titus complimented the happy recipients upon their exploits in appropriate panegyric, and decorated them with costly badges. To some were presented golden coronets, to others golden necklaces, to others golden spears, to others silver ensigns, and all were advanced a step by way of promotion in the army. The spoils taken from the enemy, gold and silver and vestments and valuables of infinite variety, were distributed in profusion amongst the troops. Titus wished them all happiness, and, descending from the tribune, offered sacrifices to the gods for the brilliant success of his arms. Herds of oxen were slaughtered on the occasion, and all the troops were feasted. The banqueting was continued for three days, and then the army broke up. Titus, with the 5th and 15th Legions, took his departure for Caesarea- on-sea. The 10th Legion, with a few auxiliary cohorts and some squadrons of horse, was left under the command of Terentius Rufus, to keep guard for a time over the ruins of the city. The 12th Legion, as the least meritorious from its former flight in the time of Cestius, was ordered for service to the banks of the Euphrates.[1]

Shortly after the departure of Titus, an unexpected incident occurred at Jerusalem. The sentries were on guard as usual on the site of the Temple, when, at dead of night, a ghost-like figure, clad in white, emerged from the ground. The first impulse of the soldiers was to flee away in terror, but second thoughts reminded them that this spectral appearance must be some artifice of the enemy, and, resuming their courage, they drew near and interrogated their unearthly guest. He declined answering except to the commander-in-chief. A messenger was despatched to Terentius Rufus, and on his arrival the figure announced himself to be Simon Bar-Gioras. On the capture of the last stronghold he had descended, with a few attached followers and some stonemasons armed with the tools of their calling, into one of the subterranean recesses, and it was hoped that before the provisions which they took with them were ex-

---

[1] 7.1.2

hausted, a passage might be excavated underground beyond the cordon of the Roman sentinels. All went well so far as the ancient vaults extended, and the workmen then began to mine; but the rock was hard and the men enfeebled, and little progress had been made when the supplies failed. The alternative was either certain death by famine, or the chance of life by a return to the open air; and Simon, choosing the latter, re-ascended, guarding himself, however, from instant butchery by assuming the character of a spectre. As the headquarters of Simon had been in the tower of Phasaelus, it is likely that he had entered the conduit, which is still traceable for a considerable distance in an eastern direction towards the Temple, and must once have been connected with it. How else could Simon have buried himself in the High Town, and have reappeared on the other side of the Tyropoeon, on the site of the Temple in the Low Town? Terentius Rufus put him in chains and sent him to Titus at Caesarea, by whom he was forwarded, with John of Gischala, to Rome, to figure in the coming triumphal procession.[1]

The reader must now transfer himself to Rome. At dawn on the day of triumph in the following year, the streets and steps of the temples and even the amphitheaters (for the procession was to pass through them) were thronged with people; and on every vacant space the platforms, which had been erected with rows of seats carried to a great height, were densely crowded with spectators. All the population of that vast metropolis was collected together, and formed, as it were, the banks of a river between which was to flow the procession all the way from the Porta Triumphalis, where it was to commence, to the Capitoline hill, at which it was to terminate. First came the senate and magistrates in their official robes; and then followed the spoils of war,—the vessels of gold and silver; the ornaments exquisitely wrought in ivory; the gorgeous purple tapestries embroidered with representations of animal life and landscapes; diamonds and other precious stones sparkling and glistering in coronals and all the other forms that the ingenuity of art could suggest; strange animals unknown to Italian skies, gaily decorated, and under the charge of keepers dressed in purple and gold Then came a multitude of Jewish captives, and at their head Simon Bar-Gioras and John of Gischala, loaded with irons. How were the

---

[1] 7.2.2

mighty fallen! Next followed models in wood, some of them three and four stories high, of the cities and towers captured in the war, and all of them glistering with gold and ivory and purple tapestries. The victorious progress of the Roman arms was represented by gigantic scenic paintings. Here was the enemy's country desolated by the ravages of the invader—there were the mortal strife and the foe put to the rout. Here were battering-rams playing against lofty towers—there were the Romans rushing up to the breach and carrying the fortress by storm. Here was the Temple of Jerusalem on fire, and there the general conflagration of the whole city. Next in order came the spoils on which the greatest value was placed—the golden table and golden candlestick and other sacred utensils taken from the Holy of Holies in the Temple at Jerusalem, and after them the Great Book of the Jewish Law used in the Temple service. Next advanced the objects of intensest attraction—Vespasian in triumphal robes, in a car drawn by four cream-colored horses, followed by Titus also in triumphal robes and in a car of similar character. Last of all came the troops in martial array, with colors flying and bands playing, chanting their paeans of victory, Io triumphe!

Hour after hour was consumed, as with slow and solemn pace the triumphal procession moved along from the Porta Triumphalis, in a tortuous course through the streets and theatres, and in front of the palaces and temples. At length it was seen ascending along the Via Sacra, and up the Forum, until at the foot of the Capitoline hill it came to a halt. At this part of the ceremony, the general of the vanquished army was to be led to the block. This painful preeminence was awarded to Simon Bar-Gioras, as the more prominent and energetic of the two chiefs. With a halter about his neck, and torn by scourges at every step, but with a haughty mien, unbroken even by this ignominy, he was led to the place of execution. The assembled multitude waited in breathless silence until the death-stroke should be announced. The signal was hoisted that Simon Bar-Gioras was no more, and one universal acclamation of triumph rose to the skies. The procession mounted slowly the Capitoline hill, and sacrifices were offered to the gods for this glorious termination of a long protracted war.[1]

John of Gischala, more fruitful of artifice than Simon, but not

---

[1] 7.5.3

perhaps less brave, was condemned to drag out the rest of his existence in perpetual imprisonment.

The Jimmie Beller Memorial eLibrary:

- A constantly-growing library of FREE eBooks!

- Each eBook has been thoroughly proofread and completely reformatted to give you the best possible reading experience!

- New books added EVERY WEEK!

- Histories
- Biographies
- Commentaries
- Doctrinal
- Devotional
- Debates
- Sermons
- And much, much more!

TheCobbSix.com

www.ingramcontent.com/pod-product-compliance
Lightning Source LLC
Chambersburg PA
CBHW051008140626
46546CB00016B/1313